My Pennsylvania Hermitage

Jim Stapleton

My Pennsylvania Hermitage

©2012 Jim Stapleton
All Rights Reserved
ISBN Number: 978-1-60571-169-0

SHIRES❦PRESS

4869 Main Street
P.O. Box 2200
Manchester Center, VT 05255
www.northshire.com/printondemand

This book was printed at the Northshire Bookstore,
a family-owned, independent bookstore
in Manchester Ctr., Vermont.
Printed in the United States of America

For Diana
Wife, muse, editor, friend, etc.

FOREWORD

This book chronicles my eight years living by myself deep in the Pennsylvania woods. Before plunging into that story I'd like to explain how I got there. Three years before I built my cabin, I had an epiphany, one of those sudden flashes of perfect insight that light up a dark part of who you are, what you're doing. This one happened while I was studying in West Germany. The year was 1962, a late October afternoon. I was sitting in my student digs at Wilhelm Weber Strasse 10, in the medieval, walled university town of Göttingen. The town lay 15 miles from the East German border, which was patrolled, ominously, by guard dogs, search lights, and machine guns. I was living in a country recently fractured by the raising of the Berlin Wall, an event I watched with my fellow students.

What was I doing there? Studying at the Institute for Theoretical Physics, I was on an academic track that would lead me to teach the science at a college, probably somewhere back home in the States. I loved physics, for me it was not an academic discipline, much less a job. It was a philosophy of life, the answer to that perennial question: What's the world made of? What is the meaning of it all?

Does it sound like physics was a religion to me? Not far off. The problem was I already had a religion, I was raised Roman Catholic. As a student I was still with the faith, though that faith had been sorely tried on all sorts of fronts. I managed to attend mass almost daily at the Sankt Paulus Kirche, only a half block from my room.

Who else was I? An outgoing sort, leading the sociable life of a young American student exploring the excitingly different culture of Europe. So there I was: physics student, practicing Catholic, man of the world! As I sat reading in my chair by the window on that dreary October afternoon, how could I have imagined how much of my world would change in the next half hour!

I was only a few months away from my *Diplom Physiker* exams, and studying fiercely. I badly needed a break from the grinding routine, a good novel. I found Aldous Huxley's <u>Point Counter Point</u> in my pile, not exactly a quick read, rather a heady, complex story of ferment - social, religious, artistic.

I can still see myself perched at the front window, reading in the late afternoon. The house I was living in was being renovated, during the day the walls were literally coming down around me. But it was quiet now, I begin to nod, prop my feet on the window sill to stretch, then back to the book . . . something about the hero's emotional distance from the real world. Suddenly I look up from my reading . . .

You Don't Want to Teach Physics, You Don't Want Anything to Do with Physics.

Yes! No doubt about it! I have never had this thought before. I am wide awake. I go back to my reading. A few pages later, again I look up . . .

You Don't Believe A Thing the Catholic Church Stands For, You Are Not One of Them.

This is not a new idea, I've struggled with it for years, but not to act upon it. Now the message is: Act upon It! A moment later I again look up and out the window . . .

You Don't Want to Live Among Others. You Want to Live Your Life Apart.

Absolutely! Have I had this thought before? I don't even know.

The rest of the evening lives vivid in my memory. The picture was becoming clear: nothing that I was doing felt like mine, all of it urged on me by others. By whom? Not my family or teachers. No, I'd carved out this path very much on my own. But I felt a pressure, something as vague as the world's expectation for *my* life, vague but powerful enough to deny me access to what *I* wanted. This was the feeling of these insights: I had been living in someone else's dream.

And there was more to this serial epiphany. Each of these NO-messages had a positive counterpart:

> No, I don't want to continue with physics because yes I want to write - stories, memoirs, novels, poetry, I'm not even sure yet. I'd been scribbling in spare moments for years and writing gave me an inner satisfaction that science never did. Over the last couple of years I'd come to realize that I would never be creative in physics, as some of my colleagues would, but I could be creative with the written word. Working creatively - that's what I really wanted.

> No, I don't want to be Catholic, but yes I want to make up my own religion according to my own lights, my own needs. I had been reading about Hinayana Buddhism. Yes this was also a blind faith - which one wasn't? - but more sane, freer of the dogmatic absurdities I had become familiar with.

> No, I don't want to be a social animal, because yes I'd rather be alone. For the last few years I began to prefer to eat dinner, hike in the woods, play music - by myself. I enjoyed communing with myself more than with anyone else.

At the end of that day I felt intellectually exhilarated and emotionally exhausted. I had been through a lot - a rebirth, a new life full of new possibilities. So what *did* I do? I did not run out the door, hop on the autobahn, and hitchhike to sunny Italy. That came later. No, I plodded through my exams, characteristically, got my degree, minus all enthusiasm, minus any expectation that I would ever teach physics, which was nearly true.

The Roman Catholic issue was easier: I never looked back. Only years later did I enter a Catholic church again as a puzzled stranger. I rarely think about it unless someone asks and then only to shrug my shoulders.

The social liberation took a little longer. I had to piece that together. I sailed back to the States only because my plan would be easier to pull off this side of the Atlantic. After exploring various schemes, I . . . but that's the story I'm going to tell here.

One can be instructed in society,
one is inspired only in solitude.
- Johann Wolfgang von Goethe

To be nobody but yourself
in a world which is doing its best
day and night
to make you like everybody else
means to fight the hardest battle
which any human being can fight
and never stop fighting
- e.e. cummings

MY PENNSYLVANIA HERMITAGE

. . . rocking . . . rocking . . . I am quietly rocking in my sleep . . . in my dream . . . of rocking . . . rocking . . . slowly I raise one eyelid . . . I am still rocking . . . the other eyelid . . . rocking . . . . Wait a minute. I'm not asleep and I'm still rocking. Not dreaming but rocking? I raise my head in the dark . . . yes . . . I am in my cabin, in the woods, and I am . . definitely . . rocking. What's going on? A dream incursion into waking life? Doesn't feel like it. An earthquake? Central Pennsylvania is not seismically active. What?

As consciousness oozes slowly into my cortex, a more plausible answer. I lift the covers and slip quietly out of bed, tiptoe, ever so gingerly to the uphill window, lift - careful, careful - the bottom corner of the heavy black curtain, lean up to the window and peer into the predawn gloom. Staring back into my wide eye, one inch away though the thin, thin glass is the wide eye of a large black bear.

The black bear had the claws of both fore-paws locked under the floorboards and his heavy shoulder squared into the side of the small cabin. Every lurching attempt to get to the food that he smelled inside sent the building into spasms and brought his face flush against the window, where his eye met mine. Hard to say who was more surprised, I can only vouch for myself, but *he* was the one who jumped and ran twenty yards up the slope. I snuck to the door and opened it a little to peek out. He stood there a long moment and peered back at me, panting visibly in the nippy dawn air, then turned and scooted up the hill, probably the way he had come.

The bear in question was *Ursus americanus*, the American Black Bear, the common bear of the lower forty-eight states. Unlike their larger relatives - grizzlies, browns, and polar bears - they are mild-mannered and generally not aggressive. Folklore and movies have given them an undeserved rep. Chipmunks are fiercer and would be a major threat to humans except for their size. In all of my encounters with black bears, some with cubs and at close range, not one has made any move except to get away. Evolutionarily, this makes sense: our kind has been far more damaging to them than their kind to us.

This particular bear, a male by his size, probably ambled down the mountain behind my cabin in his pre-dawn scavenging, smelled the food at the kitchen corner of my house, and tried to pry the booty open as he would a honey tree. I make this guess because I often met bears in the neighborhood, often on the Allegheny Straight Ridge Trail which starts a hundred yards behind my cabin. Usually they hear or smell me before I see them hustling away.

If you bicycle in a straight line from Toledo, Ohio (where my mother and other relatives lived) to New York City (friends), halfway there you are struggling up and down the Allegheny Mountains of north central Pennsylvania. On the map it's a big bare spot, a trace of blue highways, a few scattered villages of five-hundred souls or fewer. For all these reasons I started looking *right there* in the summer of 1964 for my retreat. My first big discovery: the West Virginia Pulp and Paper Co. - long since gone the way of Saturday morning movie house serials - leased quarter-acre parcels to sportsmen who wanted to build small hunting lodges in this deer-thronging wilderness. I borrowed a map of their holdings, hopped in my Jeep, and went scouting. The woodland managers of the paper company did not hide their astonishment. I was not their typical client: I didn't own a gun and didn't want to. I was looking for bigger game. But they didn't make a fuss, at least not to me.

I found what I was looking for above a small clearing in the flood plain of the West Branch of Pine Creek about 8 miles south-west of Galeton, Potter County, Pennsylvania. The site had everything I wanted, a nearby road with an electric line, a spring, a playfield, and nobody within hollering distance. Technically I had lease-rights to one-quarter acre, but what did that mean? Millions of acres of the Allegheny Mountains would be my playground.

Map of My Cabin Site
West Branch, Pine Creek, Potter County, Pennsylvania

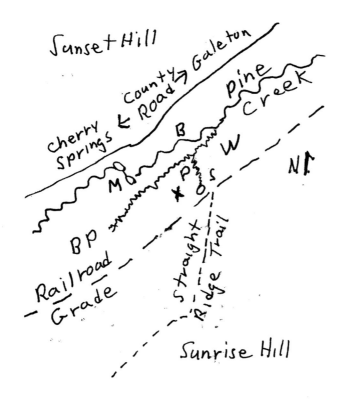

X-Cabin, P-Playfield, S-Spring, W-Woodcocks,
M-Main Bridge, B-Other Bridge, BP-Beaver Pond

First Bill for My Space in the Woods

	WEST VIRGINIA PULP AND PAPER COMPANY	
HOME OFFICE 230 PARK AVENUE NEW YORK 17, N.Y.	**W** PLATEAU WOODLANDS P. O. BOX 30 COUDERSPORT, PA.	REMIT TO: P.O. BOX 30 COUDERSPORT, PA.

INV. NO.	INV. DATE	CONTRACT NO.	UNIT NAME	UNIT NO.	PAYMENT DUE
770	7/28/64	XX	Pine Creek	8	PAID

Mr. James Stapleton
1940 Clarendon Drive
Toledo, Ohio

TERMS
Terms of Sale are governed by a contract between the Buyer and the West Virginia Pulp and Paper Company.

SPECIES	BOARD FT. OR CDS.	NO. LOGS	UNIT PRICE M&F/CDS.	AMOUNT
One-Half (½) year's Camp Site Rental, (Camp Site #39) for 1964				15.00
TOTAL				15.00
PREVIOUS BILLING DUE				
TOTAL AMOUNT DUE Paid				15.00

I was lucky in money. Most young people just out of graduate school are deeply in debt and need to get to work at once. I had a free ride to my post-graduate schooling, thanks to the German equivalent of a Fulbright Scholarship. From my long dead father I came into a small inheritance at age twenty-five, which was conveniently now. I didn't live exclusively on this, I worked sometimes for nearby farmers, haying, milking, apple-picking. But not much, because I didn't have to. I lived in those days on less than $500 a year, 1965 dollars. Those years taught me to live well but sparely, scrimping by on almost nothing, a style I've practiced ever since and which has afforded me, along with family bequests, a lifelong of uncommon leisure. I've worked for money very little and only when I choose to; when I chose not, I made do in other, richly fulfilling ways.

Mountain-need
To rest above, shadowed in silence.
Cave-need
To rest within, silent among shadows.
Silence-need
To rest from sound.
Shadow-need
To rest from light.
Ending need
To rest.

(Entries like this, in *Garamond Italic,* are from my writings of the time.)

To call these gently rounded hills 'mountains' is a stretch for anyone who's hiked in the Rockies or the Alps. But that's what the USGS calls them and according to their maps they rise here from eight to nine hundred feet above the broad valley floor which lies at fifteen hundred feet above sea level. The trees are a bewildering confusion of deciduous, evergreen, and in-betweens with the concomitant diversity of wild animal life.

A long abandoned railroad grade passed fifty yards above my cabin site, stretching from Galeton in the north to boundless woodlands in the south. This pathway proved to be the most dependable trail to get from my cabin to wherever I wanted to go. I walked it every day of my life here. Within hallooing distance to the south was an extensive network of beaver meadows which I visited often.

My cabin was not much to look at. I had dreamed a building of native stone braced by timbers from the hillside above.

My Dreamed House

Practical constraints reduced it to a prefab sheet-metal box on a lumber deck stretched over four recycled railroad ties. The single room measured twelve by twelve feet and all of my possessions and needs fit nicely inside.

Building the cabin was a test of my resolve to make this place mine. Some local boys came by to help with construction. They had heard through the vine about the New York City writer-fella building a place in the woods to live in. I remember especially two strapping young brothers, laborers from the mill two miles north. I can still see them sitting on tussocks overlooking the construction site, now and then offering help with site-clearing, carrying a beam, fetching a tool better than the one I was struggling with. I resisted every offer, sensible as they all were, even as my hands bled from ineptitude. Over the previous year of searching out my own place I had developed a certain dirty competence in fending off well-wishers. The knack served me well, the boys drifted off shaking their heads, probably sharing a few good laughs, happily at my expense.

Having led a sheltered academic life up to that time, I lacked most of the skills required for this phase of my life - wood-clearing, excavation, construction, carpentry. I learned these by doing, with a consequent high accident rate, which necessitated mastering another talent, one-handed bandaging.

There were other accomplishments, less easy to define or even label, such as learning to see in a new visual field: turning around on a trudge up the western hill to glimpse my cabin at an angle I had not even imagined, the familiar object startling and new right now. Or responding to an owl in a dark woods, hoping to learn its language by trial and error. Every twig and leaf had a story to tell if only I opened the right organ to hear it, read it.

Nothing, to my way of thinking,
is a better proof of a well-ordered mind
than a man's ability to stop just where he is
and pass some time in his own company.
- Lucius Annaeus Seneca

When I tell people the story of my Pennsylvania hermitage the question often comes up - Didn't you get lonely? - - - Yes and no. There were moments, many moments, when I longed for a buddy or a girlfriend to bullshit or snuggle with, a soul-mate to tell my story to. The possibility that there was no such soul on earth didn't staunch the tears, especially in the vulnerable gulf between unwary sleep and armed consciousness, when the most trivial traps are deviously sprung. Between these moments were stretches - days, weeks, months - when

7

I lived in a bliss of aloneness, savoring the absence of another human consciousness. Some people have told me this is sick; I felt, and feel, it is salubrious.

'Another human consciousness' above requires a note. For good or ill I find myself more sensitive to minds around me than bodies. I can comfortably stand in a packed subway until I sense someone thinking about me half a car away.

And it's not just people. When I returned from my European grand tour, I spent the winter in a cabin of a friend on the Canadian side of Lake Erie. It was a lively summer resort in August but empty in February. The only people I saw were the couple that inexplicably kept their grocery store open on a nearby provincial road. One evening a half-starved dog showed up at my door. I took him in, fed him some inappropriate table scraps I had in the refrigerator and let him curl up on a rug next to the stove. I returned to my writing. But something wasn't working, I couldn't focus on the sentence at hand. I looked down at the dog. He was looking up at me. Too close. I moved him and his rug across the room nearer the door. He didn't like this, he wanted to be next to the stove. Maybe he wanted to be next to me so he could watch. With hand and voice signals I let him know I needed him to be over there, next to the door. I returned to my work, but a few more minutes of starts and stops convinced me this wasn't going to work either. The pressure of his mind was palpable, a too-bright light in a space I needed to be dark. Reluctantly I shooed him into the cold. He slunk off.

In the early years I told one friend or relative after another, "Please don't visit, I'm not up to it." Painful as this was, the other option - anybody running anytime in and out of my psychic asylum - was not to be borne. I came to my Pennsylvania retreat with a promising sense of inner sanctuary. Up to then I had devoted my life to the "outside": success in academics, building a career, weaving a social web. Here for the first time I discovered a life within, an abundant reality independent of networks, institutions, or even other people. The longer I lived among the aspens and beavers, the richer, more elaborate, more inviting this world became. I had no one to talk with so I talked to myself. Unlike many another conversation, the longer I talked, the more I had to say. The exchange was lively, varied, and full of humor, and often unfolded in the perfect silence of a hemlock glade or the dark of my cabin.

> *Now around my mountain meadow*
> *unsoundable skyey quiet...*
> *lit still with the*
> *yet gone sun and moon-silver sliver,*
> *gracing the browsy deer -*
>
> *Oh halfway thing!*
>
> *Inbetween are two close stars...*
> *ineffably somewhere*

My conversation with myself spilled over into colloquies on the railroad grade and along the paved road across the creek, voiced in a low growl or shouts of intense feeling. One evening I was returning along the road from a long amble up the West Branch. As usual I was holding forth in a loud voice about one thing or another. As I turned off the road to drop to the level of my main bridge, I caught sight of a lone fly fisherman working the pool above the bridge. The usual clue to a human presence on the creek, a parked car, was nowhere in sight. He'd been well within earshot of my declamations of the last few minutes. How to handle this? I needed to get by him. I could have marched right along with a perfunctory 'G'd evening!' Or I might have stopped, frankly owned that I blabber to myself more or less all day long, maybe get his views about the psycho-social implications of this behavior. I had to think fast, I was still on the path . . . now or never. I turned on my heel, cupped my hands around my mouth, and hallooed up the road into the empty dusk -"O.K. Henry, see you tomorrow then!" I trotted down and hopped across the bridge with a nonchalant wave. He waved back.

Another common reaction to my hermitage story is a casual, "Boy, if only I had a chance - *i.e.* the money, time, etc. - I would *love* to do that." I doubt this with the same clarity as I do the 'sick' business. Most people I know could not bring off eight years of hermitry - it's too hard. Human life, in this era at least, is so militantly geared to the social model, heroic effort is required to live against the grain. The chief reason I held out in forging my wilderness time was that I wanted it so badly.

In reflecting on my own swimming-upstream life story I am put in mind of a scene from my youth: I am five years old , riding my tricycle up and down the sidewalk in front of our house on Homewood Avenue, Toledo, Ohio. The trike was clearly a hand-me-down, perhaps recovered from the town dump - the crude silver paint job, the wobbly wheels - and soon developed a peculiar malfunction: the pedals on the crank got turned about so that instead of opposing each other, allowing the left and right pumping action to alternate, as they're designed to do, they became aligned, requiring both feet to push together on the same stroke. The effect was that I *rowed* my steed jerkily down the sidewalk rather than pedaled it smoothly. I loved it. Mine was the only trike on the block that had so distinctive an action. Little did I realize it was probably the only one in the state of Ohio. I spasmodically propelled my little 3-wheeler from Berdan Ave. to Hillcrest Blvd. with enthusiasm that I can still taste seventy years later. Contrary motion! Alas the delight was short-lived. A well-meaning neighbor, doing his good deed for the day, pulled me over one Saturday morning, tut-tutted about my 'backward wheel', and fixed the problem with his crescent wrench. Had I known how, I would have reset it my way, but the inner meaning of 'backward' was not lost on me.

Throughout my stay at the cabin I did have regular contact with human beings. This is how it went: Every month I toiled by bicycle the twelve miles into Galeton for groceries. I did my shopping at a tiny storefront Grand Union Supermarket. The manager and only employee was a weary, Vaseline-haired man whose inner life I failed to imagine. Nonetheless we developed a dependable interaction which

10

served us both. I would walk in; he would say, "Nice day" or "Not too nice a day", depending; I would reply "Yep" or "Nope", depending. Until next month.

My other business was at the bank. I never did have much business there, a savings account from which I took out a few dollars every now and again to buy the cheapest groceries I could find at the Grand Union. I walked in . . . in my clothes. All the tellers would look at me. These rural folk are very polite. They were clearly thinking something because all of them looked up at me at once and seemed unwilling to take their eyes off of me. Was it a security question or simply a human interest story, something they could tell their grandchildren if things got that far? Civil as they were, what *were* they really thinking?

There were less regular but more expansive contacts. One mile along the railroad grade to the south lived an old gunsmith, Byron Cottrell. He was a great help in getting me started in my venture. He advised me exactly where to place the cabin to avoid the worst creek floods, which advice turned out to be exactly right. He would occasionally drop in to visit. Occasionally when I was in the mood, I would stop at his house and chat, mainly about local lore: what animals roamed these woods; how many people inhabited the meadow in front of his house in 1900, then named Corbett, Pennsylvania; how often and how badly the creek flooded. He was a rich fount of the information I was thirsty for. From Byron I learned I had built my cabin on a bear run and my playfield had been a forest potato patch decades before. We listened to music on his new hi-fi system. He had recently discovered the beauties of the classical repertoire and I shared with him what I knew of that. Regrettably his time with me was short, he died of a fall in his house a few years after my arrival.

The other neighbors were Appalachian mountain people, unkindly known as hillbillies. I soon learned there are hillbillies and hillbillies. I met some who fit the common image - rough, angular men, whom you did not want to cross in any arena. I did not even glance at their womenfolk, even now I cannot conjure a picture of

11

them. And there were friendly, decent people like Wayne and Eleanora Burrous, who happened to be born here, but could easily be mistaken for decent, friendly folk anywhere. Wayne was retired from the highway department and raised a small herd of beef cattle. I began my sinuous - up and down - career as a farmhand haying for Wayne.

I didn't think much about it at the time, but I'm sure the whole community considered me a nut case. From toddlers to dodderers these were hard-working, straight-thinking folks. And here I was, in the prime of life, hitching up trees to snoop on owls, biking into the sunset practically naked, mooning over salamanders. And they didn't know the half of it: "Ananonaninny", for instance. One of my many games, this one took place during my frequent midnight walks along the rural mountain roads. A car approaches, signaled by a flickering light in the treetops above me. I dive frantically over the gully edge milliseconds before the car whizzes cluelessly by, a few feet from my head. "Ananonaninny, Ananonaninny!" I whinny into the night, celebrating my escape from The Throng Bazooka.

Sprinkled throughout this narrative are stories of the animal and plant neighbors at my woodland cabin: bears, mice, red cedars, ferns, chickadees, and so forth. There were human visitors as well, some casual and others whose stop-overs were planned.

On a couple of occasions my older sister Rita brought a carload of her kids to my cabin. On one memorable visit, she brought our mother, Coletta, as well. Rita was a phenomenon and would require a treatise of her own to do her justice. Suffice it to say that she raised six children after her husband died in a fishing accident, then loaded her truck to drive across the country to spend the next decade of her life at the Esalen Institute where she became head of the intern program. She spent the following ten years traveling around the world giving workshops on personal empowerment. She died a few years ago after a brief bout with Parkinson's.

Needless to say when Rita showed up my carefully constructed reality fell into shambles. Things got lively during those visits, not least at night when a cabin tightly designed to sleep one became the bivouac for a half-dozen. This is best left to the imagination.

The "loose cannon" factor alluded to above was the appearance of my mother on the scene. How to paint this picture? Coletta did not approve of my career choice as hermit. She insisted, against all the evidence, that I was merely taking a breather from my meteoric business career, never mind that I had not once evidenced any inclination or aptitude for business. She did not consider academia 'business', it was only another variety of fooling around. So I was more than an enigma to her. Her visits were in some sense an attempt to figure out how I still might make money which was, after all, one's mission in life. Rita, who bore Mother more animosity than I did, mischievously connived to facilitate these inspections into the depths of my degradation. I was in on it as well - I could have said no.

The merriment was rich and parti-colored when Rita's kids showed up. They knew how to have fun. We visited all the local curiosities and made ourselves obnoxious wherever need be. Rita's son Mike was the card of the lot. Besides constructing for me a make-shift privy he busied himself drawing zany pictures with titles like "Uncle Jim is a hermit and Grandma says so!" More consternation.

Uncle Jim

Mike's Drawing

From this remove it is hard to say whether the presence of my mother enhanced or detracted from the merry-making. She certainly disapproved of pretty much everything we did. On the other hand she unwittingly supplied a handsome portion of the material for fun. My chief recollection from the visit: minutes after their departure a barred owl delivered his clarion 'YEOWLL' from a nearby branch. My bowels froze. "Oh my God, she's coming back!"

The other set of planned visitors were my friends from New York City who helped in preparing the site and made the odd summer sojourn to see me along the venture. Leave-taking from such week-end visits were always bitter-sweet, made poignant by a long shuffling walk to undo the knots and refill the spaces, to reflect how empty, how full my life was. One autumn I brought their young son, Matt, for a two week outing, just the two of us. We bicycled the roads and tramped the woods, made dinner together and participated in the evening solemnities of the beaver family. The time we shared is still warm in my memory

Many people have asked, with various degrees of delicacy - What did I do for women at my hermitage? I usually put off the question to protect the guilty. But at this remove I might as well tell the whole story . . . well, part of the whole story. I did "do" for women, but not any of the wives/sweethearts of the local hill-people. I had heard the stories. My girlfriend was from my home town, a childhood flame from elementary school days. The assignations mainly took place away from my cabin, on visits to here or there. I was after all, trying to divest myself of foreign alliances, foreign in this case being 'whoever is not me'.

Unlike many men in their twenties and thirties I never felt completely consumed by my hormones. In fact sex, with or without a partner, engaged little of my time. I used to conduct experiments to gauge the effect of abstention on my creative, *i.e.* writing, life. Opera singers are old hands at this. I remember concluding there was something to it: I wrote more energetically with a little charge in my lower belly, but as the charge built, the energy became increasingly frenetic and distracting. Whether I wrote better or worse with this discipline, the memorative trace does not record.

I am fond of making distinctions in the absence of differences, the legacy of my early exposure to Thomistic philosophy. For instance I just now wanted to make a distinction between the 'useful' and the 'playful' arts at my hermitage, but what does that mean? Snow-shoeing and tree-climbing with leg spurs were play for me, I suppose. But I profited from both, gaining such physical insights as how to move evenly on even ground or where to look upon the world from a high inner place.

I came into the woods a biological innocent. I had never had a life science course, grade, high, or higher school. Not only did I know nothing, I had assumed it was not worth knowing: knowledge was science, physics was the test of science, and biology failed the test.

Physics had the world by the short hairs with its canonical equations and pithy summations of what was going on in the world. So I came to the woods ignorant of tested biological theories and unaware of the latest prejudices, specifically the then current reductive presumption that animals were machines. With artless eyes on beavers, chickadees, and bears, I saw of course that this was not true. They are much more like us than machines are like either. So I was spared that chapter of my education. I have sometimes been accused of anthropomorphizing my encounters with fellow animals, but I ascribe this to my ignorance of the current dogma.

Overarching these steep learning curves was the gentle slope, the life skill required to create my own life there in the Allegheny wilderness, doing it, whatever 'it' was, the way that felt right for me. In writing this I am aware of another set of skills that I perhaps acquired, perhaps not. That is, the set that I am unaware of. What profundity transformed me in my eight years of hermitry that I am unable to say, suggest, even point to dumbly. I don't know. But the gnawing suspicion won't let me dismiss the possibility, the probability. It elevates and defeats me in regular turns of mind.

The inside layout of my cabin was straightforward. My only door faced north overlooking the playfield, the two windows looked east and west, uphill and down. To the right of the door was the 'kitchen': a crusty card table with plate, cup, bowl and electric frypan, all under a crude rope-slung shelf piled high with staples. There was no refrigerator. I found a spring above the playfield which served as a sort of ice-box. More than that I discovered that foods require much less refrigeration than modern American culinary science would have us believe. I was sick only once, from eating a sandwich with bread so green with mold I could no longer make out the kind of grain.

To the left of the door in the northwest corner was my writing desk, pads of yellow legal paper, and a stockpile of endlessly recycled fine-point ball pens. Hard to say which received more resuscitation work, the pens or my accident-prone tensor desk lamp. On the wall of that corner were dozens, sometimes hundreds of little notes to myself, outlines of the current opus, notable quotes, lifter-uppers, etc.:

The pace of the writing ought to be that of time itself - zipping along in quick short chapters (the day-to-day), clackity-rapid dialogue (train-ride), lapping along evenly (raft trip), long, drawn-thin, slow-paced (I dream).

Is and Is-not - are they clear poles? Oneness behind the distinctions, the creative impulse, the playful, gameful Source, from which all the distinctions are made, fictile.

A steep slope from the common sense view of things to an infinitely expanded and liberating one, from seeing things as men describe them to seeing them as men cannot describe them . . Stolen from Thoreau

Next to the table on the west side was a sheet metal woodstove I bought at Devlin's Hardware in Galeton and next to that my main piece of furniture, a broad, overstuffed Castro convertible chair-bed. The chair was ideal for curling into winter evenings, and the bed for sleeping through the year. Apart from a straight-backed kitchen chair at the desk, the Castro was the only sit-on surface in the cabin. I bought it well used for something under $50 on East 125th St. in Manhattan and, though long gone, it remains one of the durable bargains of my life.

Hanging by a rope from the ceiling in the south west corner was the cello I acquired in Göttingen as a parachute in face of my final exams. I schlepped it all over Europe and finally here. Under the cello a music stand and piles of scores. Along the south wall I stacked books and mounted a Heathkit hi-fi I put together in my high school years. The place may sound crowded but apparently not crowded enough because in my second winter, just for the hell of it, I bought a Zuckerman harpsichord kit from his Greenwich Village workshop in New York City. How I got it to my cabin I can't remember, but after laboriously screwing and glueing, sanding and staining, stringing and voicing the instrument through the long winter nights, it more than occupied the southeast corner until the cabin was dismantled fourteen years later.

My cabin had no facilities of the modern American sort. no bathroom, no track lighting, no running water except when, on occasion, the flat roof buckled under the weight of mountain snow and thin streams of icy water poured from the ceiling, often as not on my sleeping body.

A memorable insight occurred one morning as I was rummaging through the top right hand drawer of my desk, past the aspirins, toothbrush, washcloth, sewing kit, screwdriver, socket wrenches . . . Wait a minute! This same drawer holds the physical tools ministering to my inner organs, skin, clothes, furniture, and house. It covers every eventuality, from heartburn to house-burn and beyond! A continuum! Yes, a repair drawer for the whole of me!

I typically woke late, noonish. Not that I slept a lot. I often went to bed near dawn - four, five a.m. or later - especially in the summer when it was pleasant to while away the sultry nights. I remember often sinking into slumber through a rising tide of dawn. Much of my life at the hermitage was spent in the dark. I loved night. That's when I wrote, played my cello, took long walks by starlight or less. The best things happened to me at night.

Waking at my cabin, I would amble down to the stream running along the west side of my playfield and throw water on my face and chest. If the stream was frozen tight which was likely three to four months of the year I only visualized doing this. In any case, I didn't need much waking up in that season. After these ablutions I'd make myself a cup of coffee (Grand Union Instant) and a bowl of cereal (Grand Union Crunchie Somethings), and spend a moment to realize the day. The big question was: In which direction would I set out for my morning bike ride? The *direction* was crucial, it needed to be decided at the outset. The *goal* of the morning's ride, if there proved to be one, would evolve in the process. These trips - five miles to Lyman Lake or hundreds of miles across state borders - are stuff for another page.

In deep winter, especially if the roads had not been cleared, the morning ride was replaced with a morning hike, but I had to get away, if only briefly, from the scene of my unconsciousness. In midsummer the bike ride might last 'til dusk, there was that much to do.

Returning from a long, hot, summer bike trip was a sensuous moment. Aching, reeking, liquid of limb, and wobbly with delightful exhaustion, I parked my bike and threw my sweaty body into West Branch Creek, a few feet below the main crossing. Here the waters were channeled into a swift rivulet so that I had to work a little to keep my place, gently tussling with the thews and sinews of the creek for a voluptuous half hour. I look back at the scene with rushing delight, as if this were the only place in my life that I have felt refreshed. May be.

Then the languorous moment of leaving the pool, steamy-flanked, shuffling about the buzzy evening on my deliciously drained legs, dribbling the soccer ball about the playfield in aimless directions, thoughts stumbling behind.

...brazenmist of stiller airy dreams, aureoling boy, grace;
thigh lappings of laminar rushelets, lambent warm, cool -
Sun cattle lowing dream melodies along far meadows,
among fume gardens langour I, alapped, enmisted
locks ensnaring golden thighs, enamoured of bronzelove, sunardence
undulate lappeling melodied thighgold . . lovewarmth . . . dreambronzen. . . .

Dinner. I loved interesting, exotic dishes, but except for extraordinary circumstances, I could never bother making them. On my afternoon bike trips I would often fantasize dinner: beef Bourguignonne, honey walnut prawns, Cajun jambalaya, etc., etc. But when I pulled myself into my cabin for the meal, I invariably dismissed all the visions - for which I was never prepared - and opted for Uncle

19

Ben's Minute Rice, topped with a chopped Grand Union wiener, and made slippery with a can of Campbell's Tomato Soup - for which I was always prepared. There were variations on this basic dish, from the straightforward - pecans, orange slices, raisins - to the bizarre - marshmallows, Tootsie Rolls, Jujubes. None of it, apart from the odd hunk of fruit, was particularly healthful. Nor did I care. Although I enjoyed eating my crude meals, food for me at that time of my life was fuel, tanking up to run the body one more day. I look back at my dietary habits of the time with a mixture of revulsion and admiration: I was doing what I wanted to do at the time I wanted to do it. *That* could have been the inscription over the door of My Pennsylvania Hermitage. May I always live just that way.

After dinner I would take a light stroll to digest the rice-wiener-soup thing. One evening I might amble up and down the old railroad grade. Another I'd pick my way over to the beaver pond to peek in on the sundown doings of my nearest settled neighbors. It was already late, dusk or more. The beavers and I are at home.

The perceptive reader will note that I have done nothing *productive* in the American business sense this whole day. Now I state this as a matter of pride, but I'm describing events from a distance of almost fifty years. Did I feel different then? Probably not.

I note here parenthetically that my ways in these particulars - clothes, schedule, habits, housing - have changed respectably. Now, these years later, I follow at least the outward customs of the mass of mankind: rise at dawn, slumber at dusk, wear clothes, live in a real house with my wife, Diana, in a picturesque village on the verge of Vermont's Green Mountains, stepchildren and their children nearby. Themes of my previous life draw me back but only in my imagination. Life expands and contracts in unaccountable ways. I wouldn't, probably couldn't do it again.

Returning to the cabin well after dark, my *day* would begin. In retrospect I sense myself summoning the energies within me . . . to begin writing. This was the moment. Sometimes it worked; often not, and if not, I would spend the night reading, playing music, musing under the night sky. Typically I wrote the stories that had been brooding through the day. Lucubration is a three-dollar word for writing all night. I rarely did this. I parsed my prized nighttime into: writing, serious and foolish; music, listen and play; read, foreign and domestic; hike, north and south. And there may have been other things, but I have forgotten them in the rush. Then sleep, and the delicious promises every new day dangles.

In the inexplicable midnight moments,
the well-bashing, flight, and crash beauty of my inscrutable snow-poet
sings me out-of-breath.
The free and startled soul wonders
along the enigmatic course, flying scout to the dark event.
That its shape and silence are ecstasy,
no matter of every night . . .
why pretend to see, use any word?

The happy-go-lucky focus of my hideout in the woods was the playfield, a quarter acre of treeless bottomland stretching from my front door to the brooklet that drained the beaver pond. The cabin, the creek, the woods were accidental to the place; the playfield was essential. Only recently did I read Huizinga's scholarly tract, Homo Ludens, a study of The Playful Human, but I could have composed a blurb for the book back then under the fun-loving Allegheny skies.

I am a fond theorizer. I have a sandwich theory, a sex-for-sanity theory, a belching/farting hypothesis, and, to the point here, a practical philosophy of play. I have surely played since I was born, maybe before that. Being animal is being playful and the young of all species have sold their souls to play, often lose their lives for play, and here I am, as intimates are too fond of pointing out, having utterly failed at the task of growing up.

The meanest of men has his theory,
and to think at all is to theorize.
S. T. Coleridge

My kind of play bears little resemblance to verbal repartee, games hawked to computer-precocious kids, or contests pursued by muscular buckos on TV. In all of these, competition is at the forefront, the focus is on winning, often at any cost. The key words here - competition, win, focus, cost - are alien to my practice of play, which notably excludes thinking or willing, but asks for a high functioning mindlessness, a state of pure awareness, innocent of content. Paint this picture: a lone figure skates over a moonlight-frozen pond, recklessly whisking a hockey puck around a plastic mallard, now this way, now that, flowing and goalless.

I have found or made playfields at all of my homes, though they have taken many different forms. Much of my early writing and most of the works for stage that I've done in the past ten years have been about play, one way or another. One of them "Playing for Keeps" is a simple celebration of the playful spirit as I know it.

And that's the way it was at my Pennsylvania hermitage. I chose that site for its potential as a playfield and there was little to do to improve it. The windows for my cabin came in a heavy wooden crate, six foot by three. Removing one of the sides of the empty crate made it a target which I propped along the forested edge of the field. That gave me the rest of the open field to dribble a worn leather soccer ball I had salvaged from my boyhood. My circling course was not a charging drive, no cranking up for an assault, but had more the tempo of a dreamtime walkabout, an ambling examination of all possible relations among ball, field, and me, punctuated by a random loft of the ball toward the patient window box.

Mornings I would dribble across the grass and back, hauling water from the spring; later, the same, on my way to the bicycle; still later, drying off from my afternoon swim or mulling over the evening stroll along the railroad grade; and finally after midnight under the indulgent moon, around the field on a break from too much writing, thinking.

Memorable are those late evening soccer sessions, lazily nudging the ball before me in a reverie of dusky sweetness, shuffling around the field and mindless, the long gone sun only hinting at the shapes of trees. Then, a whim - loft the now no-more-than visible ball through the shadows and hearken for the satisfying 'thump' against the box. Playing in the moonlight.

> *Mistress of a long winter night of thought and the other cold . .*
> *My bash-goal pours out my soul to her,*
> *Fuse of rapport heat under the frozen stars.*
> *She, weaving under my ecstatic high thrusts . .*
> *I, goal tending soul of her crashing . .*
> *WE*

Lest one think the ballfield scene had no precedent in my past, I confess to a lifelong devotion to banging a ball against vertical surfaces. Scenes: the backyard of my childhood home on Clarendon Ave, unnumbered walls in Wisconsin, Detroit, and Germany, or the neighbor's garage in Harrow, Ontario. That is where I holed up, post Continental Tour, to reassess my prospects. The doughty weekend neighbors, good Canadians all - Daddy, Mummy and the closely held little ones - stared in huddled amazement behind their cottage curtain to watch the weirdo American pretend he was a bird floating over Lake Erie, scrawny arms flapping in wannabe flight. Everyone should have a Ridiculous Moment. I've had my share.

One feature of the soccer game I have yet to mention: in balmy weather, day or night, I romped around my playfield in the altogether. I disliked restrictive clothing. I still do fifty years later but have adjusted my habits somewhat. I slept buck naked, and looked for any excuse to wear one less garment during the day. This penchant caused no problems on my unpeopled Pennsylvania playfield, apart from one notable incident.

23

I was skipping around the grass one Sunday afternoon (only after the fact did I think to relate this incident to the Christian calendar), triumphantly unclothed. As I was rounding a drive to the window box, I looked up and glimpsed one of the most bizarre sights of my time in those wild woods. Standing on the railroad grade, well within viewing range of the game, were two stooped, grandmotherly types - purple hair, rosy print dresses, and bulky plastic purses that hung to the gravel. How these ladies got this far into the woods, I cannot guess to this day, but there they were, glued to this scene and me with all my features. What to do?

A short reflection clarified my thinking on this point: Who, after all, was out of place in this Allegheny wilderness, me or them? Case closed. *Quod erat demonstrandum.* I lofted them a hearty hand wave, turned my sweet bum to their rapt gaze, and romped away on another circuit. The next time I came around, they were gone.

I never aspired to return to nature or live the simple life, I just wanted to be alone. So it was no selling of my soul to connect to the electric grid. The only problem was that I myself had to string the line to my cabin from the electric pole on the county road. The Tri-County Rural Electric Cooperative's men installed the transformer and then tossed a quarter-mile of rubber-coated electric line and a box of insulators underneath the pole. I had no more experience in the craft of wire stringing than generating the electricity itself. After perilously screwing the ceramic insulators high onto trees by standing tiptoe on the top of my household stepladder, I scraped off a goodly amount of finger skin running the three-stranded wire through the insulators. At which point I was informed that the wires are to be fastened along the *outside* of the insulators not *through* them, a detail the electric folks had failed to mention. Back to the stepladder. Apparently I did a creditable job because the line never broke in the dozen plus years that it was up.

As much as I wanted electric power, even more so did I not want a telephone connection. I learned soon after settling in that an underground phone cable ran two feet below the surface of the abandoned railroad grade fifty yards from my house. Tapping into that line, I was told, would be the work of an hour for a line crew. I kept that dark piece of information to myself , especially in the midst of family and friends, some of whom would have loved to have access to my consciousness 24/7/365. I had to defend myself.

I hate telephones, they rank with the Black Plague as a visitation on humankind. Imagine this: a stranger steals on to your front porch and bashes on the door so insanely that you *cannot* do other than throw down your *opus magnum* and run to swing the door open, where you are pinned to the glider to listen to a four hour sales pitch for aluminum siding. Such is the telephone. Nothing good has ever happened to me on the telephone. We have one, sigh, in our present home. Not my choice. If it were, the thing would be unlisted, unknown and more often than not, unconnected.

As long as I had the Jeep I could drive south along the old railroad grade to within fifty yards of my cabin. Ironically this route was closed off by a major washout within a year of my staking claim, effectively cutting me off from motorized civilization. But I sold the Jeep as soon as I could do without it, a few weeks after the cabin was finished. From then on I did what I had to do with a bicycle and if I couldn't do it that way, I didn't do it.

Conversion to a bicycle meant crossing the creek, summer and winter, drought and flood. Therein lies a wonderful History of Bridges. Unfortunately I did not record the epic sequence of bridges I built across the West Branch of Pine Creek over the next eight years, but the number must run into scores. I chose two sites to cross the main creek. The main bridge was at a narrow neck between two pools, perhaps fifteen feet from bank to bank. In addition to a breast high rope tied to trees on each side, this crossing required felling a tree robust enough to support my weight but not so big that I couldn't position it. Ironwood (*Carpinus caroliniana*) with its tough sinewy wood was ideal for the job but since it rarely grew to more than three inches in diameter, I had to faggot two or three together for rigidity, to keep from being tossed into the creek. This was no great disaster, except when I was carrying my bicycle with panniers full of Grand Union groceries.

The second bridge was one hundred yards downstream where a mid-creek island made the crossing a little easier, two eight foot bridges instead of one twenty foot one. Here I dropped two pairs of more substantial trees and positioned the trees two feet apart over each branch. The creek itself provided an endless source of rough planks washed down from upstream disasters. I always found enough planks to form cross pieces which I nailed to the logs. With materials like these, making the bridge level, *i.e.* crossable, became a minor art form.

There was one more bridge: over a brooklet that drained the beaver pond to the south and ran between my cabin and the main stream. Here again I made a plank bridge, this one even shakier than the others. No matter, in a pinch I could throw the bike across this gap and leap over after.

Needless to say, all of these bridges washed out with a regularity that vied with the ocean tides. Any rainfall twenty percent heavier than normal would be an occasion to haul out my bridge building gear - saw, rope, hammer, and nails. A reasonable person might ask: Why didn't you expend the slight effort to build more durable bridges, thus cutting repeat bridge construction, say, in half? The answer (though it just now occurred to me) is that I *enjoyed* rebuilding my bridges. A sound, even semipermanent structure would have represented a loss of opportunity to have at the creek one more time and inevitably to be beaten by it. Sisyphus on the West Branch. One other thing: these bridges, contrary to the usual symbolism of bridges, were barriers. No person with a middling sense of physical security would voluntarily risk these crossings. Another little device to keep strangers at arm's length. When friends or family arrived I had to coax them across the bridges with feigned assurances of their sturdiness.

26

Like the streams, the trails around my cabin were unconsciously laid as paths of least resistance. In this case between points of interest: bridges, beaver ponds, woodcock display grounds, etc. One bizarre exception was the route from my cabin to the railroad grade fifty yards above. When I first arrived with my Jeep, I had to wind my way down the hill in the vehicle, weaving around aspen saplings and hummocks. The path looked like a river channel though a flat meadow. Much later, years after selling the Jeep, I was astonished to discover that I was still using the same meandering course as a foot path between cabin and railroad grade . . . mindlessly! This discovery was a sharp comeuppance. Here I was, priding myself on conducting my life *my* way, newly independent of forces beyond my vigilant conscious control, and bammo! Gross mental negligence in my own backyard.

When I built my cabin and installed a wood stove I had never heard of a chimney fire. Live and learn. One cold winter night, after several months of low level fires with subprime firewood, I decided to experiment: how big a chunk could I get into the stove, could it last the night? Unfortunately the piece I chose didn't quite fit in the top loading stove. I couldn't close the lid, but I couldn't get the chunk out. So I left it, the fire rose in the stove, burned merrily, even went a good way up the metal chimney pipe, which was becoming a cheery rose color as the open fire roared away. I returned to my reading, humming cluelessly. Gradually I became aware of a deeper rumbling, almost growling, not coming from the stove, but somehow above it, now approaching a howling. I stood up. The whole black stove pipe had turned a gorgeous crimson. I began to wonder . . . is this ok? The pipe was visibly throbbing and the fulmination, more outside than in, was reaching the pitch and volume of a Serengeti male lion call. I stepped outside. The firmament was full of fire and it wasn't stars. It was the fiery debris from my metal chimney volcanoing far and wide over the landscape, firebrands extinguished only because they fell on two feet of snow. The chimney itself looked like a test run of a rocket engine, fire shooting out a good 6 feet and spewing skull-sized embers over a radius of fifty feet. It was a magnificent display, if only I had the objectivity to appreciate it as pure phenomenon. Actually I thought the game was up with my cabin, my life in the woods. Sure, I could get away, but I might be sleeping under a bush tonight or tunneling into a snowbank like an alpine survivor, with dreams of a smoking pile of ashes fifty feet in circumference.

I was lucky. The howling subsided, the firebrands fizzled and everything returned to normal, quiet and dark. The outside chimney was in shreds, the painted sheet metal of the cabin next to the chimney blackened and blistered. The inside stovepipe looked like I could sell it to the Museum of Modern Art for a tidy sum, but nothing else was seriously damaged, a minor miracle. Most people who have chimney fires don't get off so cheaply.

Another blaze, my first winter there, equally my fault, this one to be attributed not so much to my ignorance as my stupidity. I, physicist, should have been more mindful of the laws relating electrical current to heat energy generated in a small, inadequate conductor.

This is what happened. I was trying out a new wiring plan for my cabin (I wince in recollecting the set up), but in order to test the connections, I had to hike three miles to flip the switches on the power pole across the creek. My bridges must have been washed out at the time, a regular feature of life there.

I slogged the three miles, flipped the switch, looked at the meter. "Hmmm, spinning pretty fast," I mumble to myself, "Why d'ya suppose?"

Well, just maybe there's a short in the system somewhere and electrons are banging around the inside of my cabin like pinballs in a penny arcade. Still puzzled I flip the switch off and amble back at a leisurely pace to my cabin . . .

WHICH IS ON FIRE!

28

Smoke is billowing out around the doors, windows, through the cracks in the roof. High anxiety!

I run helter-skelter down the snow-deep slope and dive into my one-room cabin choked with smoke. Flames are licking up from the far corner, the site of my electrical experiments. I stumble out, gulp a lungful of air, grab an armful of snow, back inside and dump it on the fire, then another and again and again and again. Finally the flames subside, the smoke thins enough to open the windows, I survey the damage.

Many books were burned beyond usability, some were only caramelized and some of these I still have on my bookshelf as a *memento mori* if nothing else. A few other things were crisped but the saddest was my cello, acquired in Göttingen, lovingly carted around Europe, and now hopelessly charred. I gave the parts to a violin maker friend of mine and bought another cello, but it was not the same. I never played with the same easy grace as I did my first cello. And I never diddled with a spinning electric meter again in my life.

> *He explained to me: "This thought and that thought are identical, because, you see, neither one lights up my meter."*
> *"But" I said, "I like this thought."*

Many people to whom I relate the story of my hermitage ask: Did I live completely off my own land? What sorts of fruits and vegetables did I grow there. The answers are "no" and "none". My total effort at agriculture consisted of three tomato seeds I planted in the middle of my playfield one evening, by kicking a hole in the duff with my heel and tossing in the seeds. Nothing, of course, came up. Nothing that I noticed.

I did have to store foods but I didn't do a great job of that either. I found a spring at the base of the railroad grade seventy yards from my cabin. It kept a year-round temperature of about 50°. I dug it out to accommodate a heavy steel WWII ammunition case that I found at the Galeton dump. Any item that needed to be cooler than 50° was left off my dining menu.

One last feature of the built environment was the waste disposal facility. As I've mentioned, I did not have a flush toilet. Actually I did not have a functioning toilet of any sort. My teenage nephew, Mike Rohen, who spent much of his adult life creating nifty looking spaceship mockups for B-rated science fiction movies, built a crude privy for me, no more than a perforated board over a two-foot ditch in one corner of my playfield. I never used it, it felt too confining. From the first days of my time there, even before building the cabin, I performed a daily ritual: bring a shovel to the field across my little stream, suitably distant from any water source, turn over a divot, evacuate in the fresh air, and replace the divot. Same thing tomorrow. By the end of my first fall the field was pocked with hastily turned clods, visible to the knowing eye. This system worked smoothly until the first set of hard freezes. I had failed to reckon with the state of the topsoil in the middle of winter. No divots would budge when the ground was frozen to a depth of two feet. In the following years I spent a half day in late fall digging divots that would last me though the deep cold.

Since the days of my retreat, I have found four-walled bathrooms oppressive. I will take the out-of-doors anytime, anywhere. This has caused any number of minor embarrassments behind every house I have lived in.

I am writing this at some distance from the realities I am describing: 50 years, 500 miles, and 5000 units in the other dimension. Nonetheless I have vivid memories of these times and spaces; the image of my cabin and its environs is especially crystalline. If I had any skill as a representational artist, I would paint it, sculpt it, fashion it in four, five dimensions. Well, I can at least describe it, toss a few clunky words at the memorable scene.

Because I was not interested in earth sciences at the time I don't know the name of the bedrock or soils that lay under my cabin. Interest in these realms of the natural world came twenty years later as I mapped the ecological factors of the Duck Pond watershed below Mohonk's Skytop Tower in the Shawangunk Mountains of southeastern New York. I could easily look up these Pennsylvania factoids, study their relationships with other strata, formations, complexes, but I choose not to, memorializing my ignorance as one would a locket of hair from an early, ill-fated love.

To fill out the picture I can guess that the bedrock is sedimentary, some kind of shale dotted with erratics left by one of the recent glaciations. The soils overlying this bedrock were thin and acidic, and apart from the moist valley floors, probably not good for growing much but hardy forest trees.

The hills around my cabin trended north and south, so the sun rose late over the ridge behind me and set early over the one in front. I wanted my sun day to be longer. Though I loved the night, I became critically sun-dependant in my naked cabin in the middle of the woods, as all the other animals have always been. I used to compile minute lists for what I called "Ultima Thule", lists of characteristics I would desire in a perfect habitation. A longer stretch of sun always appeared high on these lists. As compensation I remember many moving evenings of watching the sun-shadow rise on my eastern hillside . . . then blink to dusk.

The landforms were softly rolling hills, soft even by soft Appalachian standards. They were, and are, wooded in a rich deciduous/evergreen mix, delicious even to the gustatory senses. I often fantasized biting into the pistachio hillside with a half-mile mouth.

One of the best things that happened to me when I was out in the woods was that I was out in the woods. As I've said, I didn't set out to be 'in the woods'. I just wanted to be alone. But there is a certain correlation between the two which was not lost on me as I

31

pored over the West Virginia Pulp & Paper Company maps. Lucky for me, because that's the way I stumbled into the living forest with all its features and creatures. I've been entranced with it ever since.

But it was not always so. One of the downsides of my early family life was our lack of relation to the natural world. I don't remember a single encouragement to look at a passing bird, compare the trees in the neighborhood, much less observe the design of nature. Still under this pall, I spent three years abroad and brought back one image of a bird - a little brownish thing in the Canary Islands which I decided was not a canary, brown as it was.

Slowly transforming from a means to an unrelated end, the forests around my Pennsylvania cabin began to catch my eye, my mind's eye, my imagination. I began to pay attention to the life that luxuriated around me. My curiosity started with raptors, generalized to birds, expanded to bird life, and finally to life itself. Here's where I discovered trees, the dazzling mix of them in the Allegheny woods, especially outstanding in early autumn.

"Autumn" is "sadness" spelled inward,
Rustle melancholy's hue.
I too am leaving soon earthward,
Born-sad harvest . . . words untrue.

And then the variations on themes of bark, leaf, flower, and seed, their fragrances, textures, and geometry.

Every autumn
Has its moment
That holds an equal
Number of leaves
Below and above -
This is the moment.

I remember spending one afternoon sitting under a huge hemlock on the banks of West Branch Creek, tearing apart cone after

32

cone to estimate the number of seeds on the whole tree. I don't recall the figure I came up with (it was whopping) but I'll never forget the awe I felt for the prodigality of nature.

I look back in astonishment now at the time when "insects" and "mammals" were little more than concepts to me, like black holes and red dwarfs. The bird world was divided into robins, sparrows, and others. And I couldn't have cared less. In the woods I learned to care more. I bought bird books and tree and mammal guides. I spent whole mornings following deer over the mountain, whole evenings tracking the beaver as they worked their pond. I sat attentively among the trees, along the streams, around pools. I was present for the day and the night and the many splendid things they never fail to bring.

If my first love affair at the hermitage was with birds, the next was with trees. Before living in the woods my chief relation to trees were the names of streets on my daily trudge to elementary school. The Alleghenies were a revelation: here were trees, more trees, more kinds of trees in every glance above my head than ever I had noticed.

I recently found my first tree identification guide, The Trees of Pennsylvania, issued by the Pennsylvania Department of Forests and Waters. I discovered the pamphlet buried on my nature shelf behind more recent tree books. I was delighted to discover that it was chock full of notes, where and when I identified my first specimens. It appears that I found many of the fifty listed native trees within a few miles of my cabin. Some of the finds I remember to this day, like the big-tooth aspen on the railroad grade above Byron Cottrell's house. I have a tactile memory of checking the telltale size of the teeth on the margin of the leaf, the grey-brown roughness of the bark.

The index page of this book is covered with coffee-mug rings and I cannot tell now, fifty years later, whether I was happy or sad the moment I put my still damp mug on this tightly scribbled page. But I can make sense of most of the scribbling, bringing me back as close as I'll get to that sad or happy moment.

INDEX

The location notes are fascinating for what they say: 'under railroad grade, above oldest beaver pond', 'camp opposite Patterson Mill'. And what they do not: 'beneath a gray, forbidding sky', 'what a glorious day!'. I would gladly now read such peripheral notes, perhaps even relive the moment. The notes I did make sometimes evoke clear pictures: 'near my electric pole', 'below West Branch Lodge'; while others are complete mysteries: 'up Kettle Creek', 'at Siegfried Spring'.

This book was my first introduction to botanical nomenclature, here's where I met the mellifluent names - *Liriodendron tulipifera, Nyssa sylvatica,* and *Aesculus hippocastanum* - which I would sing out on my long afternoon hikes.

After trees came flowers and the rapturous language of botany: drupaceous, papilionaceous, anemophilous, malpighiaceous, rosellate, rugulose, runcinate, scaberulose, scabridulous and scabrelate. Writing these words now makes me wonder: Was I more in love with the plants or their names? But, whoa! What's the difference?

I often walked my paths in the darkest of nights, moonless with heavy cloud. I knew the ways by touch, through the soles of my feet as well as by sight. One such midnight I was stopped in my tracks by a light in the woods. Not a bright light, an eerie greenish glow, steady, unlike a firefly, but boring into the night. There would not have been another human for miles, would there. . . ? Who then was shining this ghoulish light on me?

The spooky glow froze me. Various possibilities occurred to me in quick succession, none of which sounded like they came from a scientist. After a long moment of wide-eyed speculation, I inched slowly toward the light. A few feet away I could see that it was floating in mid-air and waving ominously, an inch long, a quarter inch wide. I slid tentatively closer, reached out my hand .. touched it. It was a twig. A twig on an otherwise invisible dead bush, a twig covered with something that made it glow in the dark.

I later found out that the covering was a bioluminescent fungus, more common in the South where they call it fox-fire. I took the twig home for a closer look. In the daylight it appeared to be a very ordinary looking wood-rotting fungus. But for a few moments along the midnight path, it raised the hair on the back of my neck.

And in among the trees dwelt the birds. One December evening I stepped outside my cabin door to the higher silence of an early winter nightfall. The perfect stillness was raised a notch by the hollow hooting of a mate-seeking great horned owl. On instinct I hooted back as best I could. I had nothing planned, I had no expectation of fooling the old owl. Imagine my surprise when a dark five-foot shield dropped noiselessly from the upper valley to whish ten feet over my head. I felt rather than saw his severe eyes upon me - intruder, imposter, human! I could not unfix my gaze from the space above me for the next twenty minutes.

Great horns were not the only owls I tried to attract. As I came to know the resident birds, their music and their territories, I made an attempt to call in the other local night raptors - screech, barred, long ear, and saw whet - with varying success.

The barred owls, the most common around my cabin or at least the most commonly heard, took no heed of my calls. They believed me not a whit and I have profound respect for them on this account. On the other end of the spectrum the saw-whet owls could be pulled in at any time of day, in any weather. I had the most fun with the saw-whets, which illustrates the ancient piece of wisdom: those with whom you have a lot of fun are not necessarily the ones you respect the most.

I often heard saw-whets on my walks around the cabin, I suspected they were nesting nearby. After laborious spying I found the nest a quarter of a mile north a hundred feet below the railroad grade. The nest was thirty feet high in a cavity of a yellow birch snag, probably drilled by one of the local woodpeckers. I dearly wanted to inspect the nest more closely and went to some lengths to do that, outfitting myself with climbing spurs and ropes, the kind utility linemen use to hoist themselves up poles and tie themselves in. I did not want to climb the nest tree for fear of alarming them to the point of abandoning the nest. Another concern was that the decaying tree could snap under my weight and leave me sprawled broken on the ground. I found a sturdy young butternut tree about fifteen feet away that allowed me to peer down into the nest cavity. I climbed the butternut every day for weeks.

To minimize the disruption to their lives, I never stayed at my perch long. In any case it was not clear that my presence was disruptive. As birds go, owls are pretty laid back and saw-whets are calmer than most. These birds seemed to take my intrusion in stride. She (I assumed it was she) would follow me up the butternut with her eyes, watching from the safety of her inclosure, only her face showing. He would peer at me from a nearby branch. Both had that wistful, melancholic gaze that makes saw-whets so winning. Often the male would show up with a mouse or vole hanging from his beak. If I were in the butternut, he would not go to the nest with the prey at first. I'd have to climb down before he would risk that move. Gradually he became bolder and in a week's time he'd fly right by me to the nest after a successful hunt. He landed on the edge of the opening and in a series of head shifts executed a courtly exchange of the limp mouse from his beak to hers. He would fly off and she would slip down into the cavity, either to eat the mouse or feed it to her chicks below. I never knew for sure whether she was setting on eggs or brooding chicks.

One thing was certain: he was a good provider, there was a steady stream of small mammals to keep the family in protein. So why did I come up with the following plan? - - I would supply the saw-whets with food! What they clearly needed were mice and I had mice aplenty. White-footed mice, *Peromyscus leucopus*, inhabited my cabin with more authority than I did. In my time there I found myself conducting an all out war on them, which involved any means to keep them from running over my breakfast in the morning or my face at night. The "means" ran from verbal abuse to poisons, traps, and ambushes with deadly instruments.

I never felt completely wholesome about all this destruction of life; at the same time I never slackened my pace. It was me or them. But, Ha! Now I had a holy justification. My new mission in life was to feed a family in need, the saw-whets! Forget that they were not precisely 'in need'. They were, in fact, doing quite well, the clumsiest of them much more efficient in harvesting mice than I ever could be. Never mind! They needed me and I was ready and willing to sacrifice all to come to their aid.

I reasoned that since the owls were not scavengers but hunters, they would turn up their beaks at any dead mouse that I might bring. I had to catch them live and bring them live to the nest. This was a new challenge since up to then any mouse under my control was a dead mouse.

I then set about live-catching my household mice. This should be easy business, I said to myself, they are running all over the place. I built one live trap after another, designed either to be tripped from across the room, or, after I got tired of waiting, with self tripping mechanisms, some of them quite sophisticated for my skimpy mechanical skills. None of them worked. If I wanted live mice, I'd have to grab them and they were a lot quicker than I was.

Set back but not defeated. Maybe the saw-whets *would* take a freshly dead mouse, these I could supply *ad libitum*. I fashioned a long, thin pole from a sapling and loosely fastened last night's kill to the end. I tied the pole to my belt and climbed the butternut. Both saw-whets appeared on cue. I offered the mouse first to the male, dangling it temptingly in front of his beak, then to the female. "No thanks" on both accounts. Even jiggling the bait and squealing miserably did not lift them out of their patent disbelief.

Stymied on that front as well I returned to constructing live-trapping devices, but before I came up with a successful one, the owls left the nest probably with their new brood in tow. I vowed to resume the experiment the following spring but that was the year I started working on farms. I never saw the saw-whets again.

Another owl I had fun with was the eastern screech owl. I enjoyed trying to lure them with my own attempt at their call, not because they came which they rarely did, but because their ethereal whinnying voice was so pleasing to practice. I would sit outside my cabin in the falling dusk of early spring, working on my whinny, checking it against an occasional distant response.

Why call in owls at all? Or chickadees or birds of any stripe? When I sound the screech owl whinny in the hopes of relating to some near or distant bird of that name, there is a moment's genetic dislocation: Am I a screech owl? Despite appearances I *might* be a screech owl, if an authority, *i.e.* another of my kind, accepted me as a screech owl. But they don't believe it, nor in the end, do I. Yet I continue to play the part, to transform *as if* into screech-owl-ness just for this moment. In fact I could easily entertain a long series of moments in which I become one animal after another in quick succession, so rich is life. And at the end ask: Am I then a screech owl?

> *These electric flowers I am charged with opening*
> *are for now my soul -*
> *arc to my joy immemorably*
> *and while me...no time to say*
> *This Now.*

I was loping around my playfield one evening during my first spring when I was stopped in my tracks by a peculiar whistling and whirring in the clearing to the north. Intrigued I gingerly picked my way over the boundary stream, hunched down in the bushes, and watched in the dusk. A minute later a dark shape shot by my ear, rising, whistling. For the next few seconds, nothing. Then a wild cascade of chirping and winnowing as the shape plummeted from a far corner of the sky. Again, seconds of silence . . . before ... "Bbbpppttttff!"

Excuse me?

After repeated performances which lasted well into dark, I managed to reconstruct what was going on. Every few minutes a chunky brown bird flew up from the wet meadow and spiraled his way skyward in fluttering, twittering flight. After a long moment of being lost in the high shadow of falling dusk, he reappeared in an explosion of wild chirping, wing whistling, plummeting pell-mell down to the spot he rose from a half-minute before. Another long moment before he uttered the sound which I can best describe as a Bronx cheer, produced in the human mouth by pursing the lips tightly and blowing hard - Bbbpppttfff. How the bird achieved this effect I do not know. His mating display was magnificent in sight and sound, launching upward, lost in the heights, plunging with an ecstasy of burbles, then, after a caught breath pause -"Bbbpppttffff!" Bringing us all down to earth.

The light was so dim I had no idea what this bird looked like until I tracked him down in my Peterson Guide, narrowing the choices by his unusual behavior. He was an American woodcock, warm brown, squat and stocky. This bird has the air of a bank clerk who brings his lunch to work. How fitting that so exalted a spectacle, ending with a common belch, should be carried off by such a humdrum looking fellow. Many an evening after that I brought a chair out to sit, watch, and listen. It's that kind of performance.

Some of the birds I had to hunt down, ferret out, sneak up on. Some came to me. This was certainly the case with my phoebes. Eastern phoebes have the habit of nesting on human structures, bridges and houses. They built on my house the first chance they got, the spring of '65, and returned every nesting season thereafter.

No matter how weak your paternal instincts, when a pair of five-inch birds entrust themselves and their even smaller, more helpless offspring to your structure, your care, you become engaged, protective, even surly with anyone who might threaten them. That's how I felt about my phoebes. That's how I still feel about phoebes who graced every east coast house I lived in . . and the winter wrens who did the same on our west coast house.

One spring evening I heard someone trying to start a motorboat in the woods nearby. "Put-put-put-PUT-PUT-put-a-poo-foofoof". This made no sense at all because there is no body of water within miles that might do for a motorboat. Maybe I misheard? No, there it was again. "Put-put-put-PUT-PUT-put-a-poo-foofoof". And again. And again. A motorboat, no question about it, forever trying to start and forever petering out. It got to be exasperating. Why didn't the numskull adjust the choke, clean the spark plug, something! And anyway what kind of lame-brain would work on his motorboat so relentlessly in the middle of a lakeless woods.

Naturally I was misinterpreting. This is common enough and correctable, but a correction rarely transferable from the last mistake to the next. Nobody was trying to start a motorboat. There was no motorboat. No engine or engineer of any kind. I don't remember how I found out that it was a bird called a ruffed grouse. Every spring and sometimes in the fall a woodland walker might well hear what she thinks is a motorboat trying to start, but what she's hearing is a male grouse advertising to any and all females of his kind within earshot by rapidly beating his wings.

There is a difference between misinterpreting a keenly observed event and missing the thing entirely. I had a lot of practice in the latter. I'm not talking about paying poor attention to the world in our ambit - we miss most of it; I'm referring to what we don't see while we are deliberately looking for it and often at it. Case in point is the nest of the northern cardinal. I knew pretty well where the local cardinals were nesting: the hedgerow between my playfield and the woodcock marsh to the north. I had scared them up often enough there and heard him sing from every corner of the patch. More convincing evidence appeared every winter. After the leaves were gone I found the remains of their nest in that ten yard strip of vegetation. All this evidence went for naught next summer when I searched the same leafy scrub for anything that looked like a new nest . . . nothing! Wait 'til winter.

Have you ever met a grouse or turkey family in the woods? Mama grouse/turkey hopes you haven't. It's a traumatic moment for her; the chicks are unable to fly, but follow her around for weeks scrounging from the forest floor. I came upon them frequently in late spring and trained myself to *not* look at mama grouse flapping pitifully at my feet, but to watch how her chicks used the momentary distraction to dive under the nearest leaf or clump of grass. Then I tiptoed back the way I came. They had a tough enough life without more grief from me.

In another book, <u>Sanctuary Almanac</u>, I describe my playful experiments hand-feeding seeds to chickadees and other needy winter birds. There I outlined my sure-fire method of getting the birds from feeder to hand. I'll repeat the formula here:

1) Live in an area where there are lots of winter feeder birds, especially chickadees, titmice, nuthatches, small woodpeckers, but *not* in an area with a lot of other bird feeders.
2) Feed them generously through the winter, emphasizing sunflower seeds.
3) Wait for a bitter cold day, when they are feeding heavily, then
4) Quickly remove all seeds from the site and simultaneously
5) Place your outstretched hand full of seeds into the middle of the feeding area, while
6) Hiding the rest of your body as best you can.

Hold your hand perfectly still. Any movement will spook the birds as will an obvious connection between your hand and the rest of you, especially your mouth. Birds know what their enemies eat with. The rest is patience. But not much patience. I have won bets with skeptical friends on the time required to get the first bird onto my hand. This interval is measured in minutes not hours.

Once one bird risks your outstretched hand, others will quickly venture the move. In short order you might have a dozen birds of three or four species regularly foraging from your body. Where you go next with this new familiarity is bounded only by your imagination.

One of the more delightful ways for me to pass an evening was to mosey after dinner to the beaver pond which spread over several acres immediately south of my cabin. I would settle on a hummock a few feet from the edge of the pond just after the sun dropped over the western hill which meant there was still an hour or so of dimming light. Soon the papa beaver (or so I guessed, he was bigger and definitely the enforcer type) slipped out of the lodge and appeared at the surface, only his nose and eyes above water. For the next ten minutes he noiselessly patrolled, first in a tight circle around the lodge, then in widening ambits until he neared the shore, neared me. I could see him peering into the dusk, sniffing the evening, harking to any trouble in the domain. In his reckoning I was trouble, no matter what my feelings toward him. I always sat perfectly still, downwind if any breeze stirred. Sometimes he caught something, probably an odor, maybe the tell-tale bouquet of secondhand tomato soup. Then he flipped over forward, his paddle tail slapping the water with a crack that resounded for a mile around, a warning for all beavers in his tribe to head for the fort. At this he himself retired underwater to his lodge and would not reappear for fifteen minutes or so.

At this point I sometimes stole off leaving them in peace. Often I waited, settling back for an hour of watching the beaver family at their vesper doings, among the most enjoyable evenings I've spent. I loved especially to watch the young of the year in late summer when they would emerge well after the adults. Like the young of many species they were trusting, clueless, often meandering within a few feet of me in their search for a tasty scrap of aspen bark or a birch twig for some reason more scrumptious than the thousand others scattered everywhere. Their front paws were remarkable, more like human hands than any animal's hereabouts, but black, as if wearing tight leather gloves. And they used them like human hands, deftly manipulating the most unmanageable woody structures. But after a spell they would shuffle back to the pond, slip in, and swim for many minutes underwater, which brought me up short - "No, they're not like humans; no human could do that."

My other evening pastime was sauntering the abandoned railroad bed. I came to *know* the path, the way you know the inside of your mouth, every ridge, plush, and soreness. I fell off the path a few times, the first thousand strolls, but never in the later years. I probably stepped on any number of animals - insects, salamanders, snakes - but the only one that worried me were skunks. (There were no venomous snakes reputedly for miles around.) I came very close to treading on a skunk on more than one midnight occasion. Its scientific name, *Mephitis mephitis*, which translates roughly as double stinko, tells only half the story. Here's the other part: a striped skunk is the soul of obtuseness. Probably because of its first class defense system, nature has neglected to provide it with any brains and with only a dim awareness of its surroundings.

I encountered a lot of bears in my time at the cabin, one of those encounters begins this book. Here are some more:

One evening well after sundown and further along the railroad grade I was suddenly startled by swift shadows racing across a farm field below the trail, horses galloping through the dusk as if their life depended on it. - - Why? - - 'Why' came along a moment later: a black bear lumbering down the middle of the field, possibly unaware of the high drama ahead of him or possibly thinking a little horsemeat might hit the spot this evening. I lost sight of them all a moment later, free to construct my own scenario of 'beginning, middle, and end', which of course I did.

Late one fall I was ambling up country on the railroad grade, almost off the lands of my neighbor to the south, Wayne Burrous, when I happened to catch sight of a dark shape shuffling through the meadow. I froze. One of the very few times I saw a bear before he saw me. I waited and watched. The sizable bear knew what he was about, this particular draw was a long-abandoned farm, evidenced by a few gnarly old apple trees each with a peck of apples still hanging on at the top. Probably his great-great-grandfather knew this patch and the tradition was handed down. In any case I watched the bear mosey from one tree to another and feast. What fascinated me was his manner of getting to the top. He simply raised a forepaw to a lower branch and lifted himself, all three or four hundred pounds of him, hand over hand, foot over foot twenty feet up. He did this with so little apparent effort that he seemed to float to the top of the tree. One of those visions you carry to your grave.

Another fall, Freddy Shogum, a friend of Byron Cottrell, shot a bear on a hunt up the West Branch. In spite of his bear-shooting habits I took a liking to Freddy, he seemed otherwise a gentle old fellow. I watched as the hunting party dressed the bear, eviscerating it and peeling away its head and hide. Dangling from a scaffold in front of Byron's cabin, the remains looked considerably smaller and less threatening than in life. I was impressed nonetheless by the thick, bulging muscles of its legs. I understood then how it might easily float to the top of a tree. Freddy offered me the liver to cook which I did, but I can't recommend the dish to anyone, and I won't.

One particularly dramatic encounter: as I climbed a short steep hillock along the otherwise level Straight Ridge Trail, a medium size black bear was charging up the other side. We met at the top, maybe six feet nose to nose. We heard each other gasp. I was frozen to the spot, she had the presence of mind to gallop off the other way, but stopped and looked back from fifty yards. Assessing me a long moment, she turned and lumbered off the way she had come. So did I.

Another late summer sighting is memorable. I think I caught the essence of *Ursus americanus* in this winning scene. About one half-mile north of my cabin the railroad overlooks an abandoned beaver pond, densely covered with raspberry bushes. One evening strolling along the roadbed, I caught sight of a large dark object that wasn't there the last one hundred times I scanned the scene. It quickly resolved to a fair-sized black bear who had flung himself backward into the middle of a heavy mass of raspberry bushes. The bushes were keeping the animal off the ground and almost completely enclosing him in a bower of vines heavy with the ripe red fruit. The bear was leisurely gleaning the berries from the canes with his claws as he made wide swings of his paws through the bounty around him, pushing each fistful into his juice-dribbling mouth. He looked for all the world like a Roman voluptuary at the Festival of Raspberries. He stopped periodically to harken and sniff the air, but I quietly tiptoed farther along the path leaving him sprawled at his luxurious banquet table.

By far the most common large mammal in the area were deer. This fact was not lost on the hunting fraternity who showed up by the thousands in crinkly new duds on the first day of the season and as suddenly disappeared. Most of them hailed from distant cities and were laughable except that they carried lethal weapons they didn't know how to use. I stayed indoors on those days. In my time there I did meet a few hunters who knew what they were doing. They didn't look anything like the First Day crowd.

I saw deer almost every day at my mountain cabin and often with their button-cute fawns in early summer. One morning walking home by Byron's house a tiny fawn, probably not two or three days old, wobbled up to me and began nuzzling my hand, probably looking for something like a nipple. I was startled and concerned because the story is told that a doe will reject a fawn with a human smell about him. Another forest tale proven untrue: I saw the mother nursing her young a few minutes later.

I once heard another displaced fawn bleating piteously along the bank of the West Branch. He had wandered around a bend in the creek and out of sight of his mother. She, hearing his bleats, was stamping, snorting, and wild-eyed thirty yards around the corner. I watched the drama from the road a quarter of a mile away. A few moments later they were together. This was another Little Daily Lesson: how quickly, easily things can go awry in the forest.

When lovely lady stoops to folly
And rounds around her tawny story
From then til now in browsy feeding
Her common shame and secret glory.

When lovely lady in November
All the forest can't remember -

Forest quiet in the cold,
Lovely lady's tale untold -

Woodland murmur through the thaw,
Stirring in the lady's maw -

Buds too were babes in mother's cluster
And slept right through last winter's bluster;
But now they spring all rumpled here,
Sensing that the time is near . . .

So hurry you birds and clear your throats,
Try lulling trills, some danger notes;
By practice turns surround this place
For worldly shh and private grace.

The sun ahems the wind to rustle,
Now babble little closer, brook.
And twigs and stars, you stipplers, stipple -
Look! She's coming, looking for our nook.

When lovely lady stoops to folly
All the forest keeps her secret.

Muskrats were a frequent presence. They lived along the creek and built crude stick lodges in abandoned beaver meadows. I often saw them swimming in a pond or creek carrying a twig or leafy plant in their mouths. A memorable encounter occurred one evening as I was coming back from a late evening stroll on the road. Just after I crossed the double bridges I heard a quick scuffling off to my left. One second later I felt a muskrat frantically climbing my leg, no doubt mistaking me for a route to safety. In no time at all he realized his mistake, dove off my leg, and scampered into the shadowy stream. I'm sure the creature was at least as shocked as I was.

I saw many fewer foxes than were actually running through the mountainous woods above my cabin. This applies of course to every animal, but especially to the cagey ones like foxes. Sometimes I found fox sign: a scat, fine red hair on a shrub, or a telltale delicate footprint in the snow. Only rarely did I see the animal itself.

I was taking a twilight stroll south along the old railroad into Wayne Burrous's pastures the landscape that had been a flourishing railroad town seventy five years before. I turned a corner and froze in my tracks. Fifty yards ahead of me a red fox trotted out of the woods and sniffed the air. He hadn't spotted me because I was downwind and not in his field of view 'til that moment. Hooray! This makes up for all the times such encounters have gone the other way. For the next few minutes I had a candid camera view into the life of this wiliest of wild animals. I watched as he trotted diagonally across the meadow, the definition of alertness, stopping here and there to check out a promising scent, a likely patch of upturned soil. After a bit he stopped and settled back on his rear haunches. Very much like a dog, I thought. And why not? He is in the family of *Canidae,* just like all the other dogs in the world. But then he did something that I will repicture into my senility. He bent over to his right, stretching his nose forward and with his right hind foot scratched vigorously under the shoulder joint of his right front leg. Exactly like a dog, like every dog we have ever watched have a good scratch under the ribs. I was enthralled! In a flash intuiting the continuity from the wildest of the wild, this red fox, to the tamest of the tame, some Park Avenue lap puppy rising from her silk pillow to satisfy a dainty itch. Yes! He trotted back into the woods; he never saw me watching; it was a good spotting.

On summer nights the soundscape around my cabin was rich with the music of insects, night birds, and soughing trees. One of the most comforting of the night sounds was made by the bats. Bats are not known for audibly vocalizing although I did hear a bat squeal once as I held it in my hand. The bats around my cabin belonged to the genus *Myotis,* small brown bats that make their living on the wing snapping up insects in the late evening. They were fond of my cabin

48

because the light from the windows attracted a lot of flying insects. The bats would cruise in tight circles around the house picking off bugs at every turn. As they flitted by, a wing would often whisk against a corner post, creating inside a patter of bat-wing whisks. This whispering was unaccountably reassuring to me as I sat writing at my desk: yes, all is toward in the forest.

My experience in the woods was by no means exclusively with warm-blooded animals. There were no poisonous snakes around my cabin or rather no one ever met one, including myself. This made my midnight rambles a bit more easy-going. My sole encounter with a rattlesnake occurred on a long bicycle trip I took to the northwestern corner of the county. I had cycled up a steep hill with a fire lookout tower at the top. I was circling the tower on its dusty service road and peering up to see if anyone might be in the cabin on top when I heard an ominous buzzing at my toes. Stretched out from my front tire to the back was a huge rattlesnake, inches from my scantily clad feet clipped into the pedals. One brief moment of panic before I realized the head and tail of the snake had been cut off not long before, the buzzing came from flies visiting the still bleeding wounds.

The other cold-blooded animals that figured prominently in my hermitage were the red-spotted newts, a species of salamander that slid from pond to road to pond, appearing everywhere I strolled. I found it hard not to step on them, especially after dark. In fact I composed a story about them, or about vulnerability, which I have included with other stories in the Appendix. This much abbreviated tale, like many others, was written under the thrall of Kafka. Who *are* these salamanders? Who am I? I confess I don't know and am confident I knew even less at the time. One sure thing: I didn't know much about salamander biology back then.

I have lived my life largely sauntering in the Kingdom of Imagination which may explain my lack of interest in matters corporeal. It is conventional to dismiss such a life as escapist, but I have always accepted it as another way to be. There are many ways. Several of my lives have passed through my body, many more in my fancy. Upon reflection, especially distant reflection, the two streams merge and fluidly become one. Did that happen? Or did it *happen?* Never mind. No matter. It is mine.

When I dwelt in the woods it did not occur to me my fantasy life was beyond the ordinary. Only years later when Diana plied me with questions - 'What are you thinking about?' 'Where are you now?' - did we discover the compass of my mental extravagations, far beyond her own process and that of others whom I later questioned. Here's a sample from a real car trip about 1990, on a real road, US 101 east of Sequim WA, shortly after passing a Chevy compact in the westbound lane carrying an elderly couple and pulling a small U-Haul trailer. A real question - "Where are you now?" - brought forth this other-real response:

> In another space (not Hwy 101) I wheeled our car around and followed the couple to their home in one of the dreadful, newish developments north of Sequim village. As they, Clarence and Alva, pulled into their driveway, I stopped in front, ran up to introduce myself, inquire whether I could be of any help with moving whatever was in the trailer. Yes indeed, it was a dining room set from nephew Gregory who was moving out of Seattle. What with Alva's back and the new pacemaker in Clarence, they weren't sure about getting the doggone thing in the house. We did get it in just before a light rain shower and had a pleasant cup of tea and scones on their rattan-sided patio, reminiscing about Ohio.

One other Big Question friends posed about my stay in the woods was: Why? The question is straightforward, the answer has circuits. Different motives for staying evolved the longer I stayed. A few years before I found the place the rationale for going was given to me in the serial epiphany described in the foreword. Years of living the expected life in the academic, social, and religious realms turned yellow one autumn afternoon in my Göttingen digs. I needed to take my own bearings, to create myself. I did. I liked what I did and never looked back. The longer I lived in the woods by myself, the fuller the experience became, as if in dredging a spring I had tapped a vein of sweet water and sat sipping the heady liquor long after satisfying my animal thirst.

Most people have some social tendencies. They want - like horses, mice, and ants - to be with their own kind. There are advantages to this preference documented by evolutionary biologists. Some philosophers have tried to justify this visceral impulse with a generalizing rationale: "Man is a social animal", "The perfection of man is in the social sphere", etc. This tends to disqualify anyone with a different visceral impulse. Like me.

Now Here is nowhere;
Is 'n O!
Where isn'?
Ow!
Here!!

While writing this memoir the thought has occurred more than once that my stay in the Alleghenies was a recovery from childhood. Some seem to have no need to recover from childhood. Many do it with a child of their own. Others require a lifetime and even then never quite pull it off. Perhaps I needed the days, many days it turned out, in my Pennsylvania cabin to scramble from that pit. The theory is: if my first childhood is botched, I'll recreate the scene to do it better the next time around. If this is true I spent 8+ years at the task, the usual span of a post-infancy childhood, in creating the wonder anew.

A good friend of mine, Len Atkins, former owner of the famous Sou'wester Lodge in Seaview, WA, once offered another insight into what I was doing in the Alleghenies. After I presented a few of the stories above to a Sou'wester audience, Len described my time in the woods as a "spiritual odyssey", a mythic going into the desert or mountains, as did Buddha, Christ, and Zarathustra. I certainly never thought of it that way while I was there. I felt rather that I was escaping from what I then perceived as the spiritual. In fact I had never thought of my alone time that way until he said it. Yet his description rang a bell and still resonates.

Living free of social pressures allowed me to wear whatever I wanted and I did . . . or rather, I didn't. Depending on the season, I didn't wear very much. Summers are warm and lush in the Alleghenies and I quickly discovered how little I needed to stay comfortable: underwear and socks were the first to go, then shirts and often shoes. In and around my cabin, summer apparel often disappeared altogether, but on hikes and bike rides, I kept this side of the Potter County decency ordinances with a pair of paper-thin surplus army fatigues, bitten off at the knees. As the pair wore away over the years I would patch them with whatever was at hand, usually remnants of garments that had otherwise completely disintegrated. I always had a supply of these. In retrospect my wardrobe consisted of rags. At the time I thought of them as clothes.

I have no recollection of bringing my clothes to a laundromat in Galeton, if there was such a business, or of washing them next to the stream. I must have done *something* like that but it's not a certainty. I do remember bathing and swimming in the pool of Pine Creek just below my principal bridge. I may have done this in stages: fully clothed, in the way of laundry, then fully unclothed, as a bath. My memory is clouded on these details. In any case splashing in the pool was strictly a warm weather affair. To keep clean the rest of the year, I sloshed water on my face at the brooklet that edged my playfield. What I did when that froze solid is anybody's guess.

For bicycle trips, especially long camping trips, I developed a minimalist approach to clothing. One prominent feature of this was my "attach-a-pants". Rather than carry two pairs of pants, shorts for riding and a longer pair for cool evenings and mornings, I snipped off a pair of army fatigues above the knees and carried the bottoms in my bedroll. After a long day of pedaling I would look for a comfortably remote spot to camp, pull out the bottoms and attach them to the shorts with 4 large steel safety pins. I note that Eddie Bauer® now sells pants of just this sort, not held together by safety pins but with sleek nylon tuck-away zippers. Their advertising makes no mention that this handy product was invented fifty years ago in the back roads of the Allegheny Mountains. Nor to date have I received a single patent royalty from the Bauer organization. This is not remarkable as I have yet to file my infringement claim.

In the winter bicycling could be hazardous in the snow-belt Alleghenies and I used heavy clothes as a defense against hitting the pavement after skidding out of an ice rut. One particular morning I put on several pairs of pants, but I ran out of belts. Since the outermost pair was the floppiest and most in need of support, I simply tied a hempen rope around it at the waist, Pappy Yokum style. In town that day a neighbor I knew asked me for some piece of information that happened to be in one of the inner pockets. Somewhat unconscious of the spectacle I was making of myself there on Main Street, Galeton, I wrenched up my three layers of pullover sweaters revealing the floppy sweats securely tied with the scraggly rope. Only after I spotted the neighbor's stricken face did I get the whole picture.

I have told the following story to friends over the years and they laugh and scold: 'That's a fun tale, but of course it's not true.' Let me step aside at this point to say I have made every effort to stick to the facts in this narrative. However, I *am* recalling events of half a century ago, and incidents at this distance *do* tend to take on a flavor, especially the details of oft-repeated tales. The following story, however, has the authority of gospel, because, more than anything, it remains so vivid in my recollection,

53

Winter in my little cabin was hard, it was an ongoing challenge to keep warm. Nights would often drop well below 0⁰ Fahrenheit with 2 or 3 feet of snow covering the world outside. In wake time I could huddle near my wood stove to read, write, or play music, but while sleeping the fire would inevitably go out and I would wake with a circle of hoarfrost around the breathing hole in my sleeping bag a few inches from my mouth. On more than one morning I awoke to find the pan of drinking water I kept on the kitchen table a solid rock of ice.

So I learned to prepare for winter. My first line of defense were the clothes on my body. Sometime in late autumn I would notice that it was uncomfortable to slip off my purple tee-shirt before crawling into bed. The purple tee-shirt stayed on. Not long after that the nippy air suggested a flannel shirt would also be comfortable for sleeping. The flannel stayed on over the purple tee-shirt that night and the days and nights thereafter. The same iron necessity followed with the light pullover sweater, the heavy pullover, and finally in the darkest moment of winter, the down jacket, each garment enclosing the previous. Here I huddled inside for weeks . . . until the earth creaked on its axis, the sun inched slowly higher in the southern sky, warming days by still frozen nights. Sometime in a late January moment of thaw, I stretched in the warmth of my wood fire and took off the down coat. Weeks later I risked wrenching off the heavy pullover. As spring approached, away with the light pullover and finally the April day arrived when I felt strong enough to unbutton - one triumphant button after another - the flannel shirt and peel it off my body. The purple tee-shirt was gone!

As to conforming outwardly and living your own life inwardly,
I do not think much of that.
-Henry David Thoreau

I never had need of a physician the entire time at my cabin. I was sick to my stomach once, got a cold or two, felt a little unwell probably no more than half a dozen times. I've always had a scrappy

54

immune system but no doubt the rigorous living conditions contributed to my robust health. I was living with vectors a lot tougher than bacteria.

The one exception to this was my teeth. I've had crumby teeth since early youth and it's probably genetic: My mother lived with none of her own teeth for more than half her life and my father died before his teeth had a chance to rot. I visited a dentist two or three times during my stay in the woods, by far the most medical attention I had. One story survives: My bicycle served for more than getting about - it had the only mirror I possessed. One day as I was about to take a spin, I mugged into it, playing Jimmy Cagney or Casey Stengel or somebody, and discovered to my horror a huge hole at the gum line of one of my front teeth. The hole appeared to be half the size of the tooth, maybe more. Nothing like a visible hole in your tooth to give you the quick willies. I promptly pedaled over to the nearest dentist in Mansfield, Pennsylvania, forty miles away. I recall the circuitous phrases I needed to explain exactly where in that bear-thronging wilderness I lived and why my cabin did not have a telephone or even a street address. He asked me to pay on the spot and I don't blame him.

Like most American children I owned a bicycle as a boy. I used it as most American kids did in those days: back and forth to school, labor to the corner grocery for a bag of flour, whiz to the local park for a tennis game, rendezvous with my pals for some random act of mischief. As a boy, I never considered my bike an end in itself, valuable as a life experience. Thus the revelation of 1964. Soon after settling into my cabin in the woods, I traded in the Jeep and bought a 3-speed bike from the Galeton Western Auto store. True, I did use it for practical purposes, hauling groceries from town and occasionally carting trash back to the landfill. But these were the least of its uses, and even then I savored each trip as a pretext to study the minute developments of the twelve mile route - watching the corn grow in the fields, counting the ospreys on the dead snags over West Branch

Creek, looking out for rattlesnakes stretched across the road - all with high expectations.

But the real use of my new bicycle lay in the other direction, along the empty country lanes not drawn on Pennsylvania highway maps. Every morning after breakfast I would hop on my bike and ride out. Wherever I rode was *good* to bike to and I often came back freshly exhausted just before nightfall.

I loved to set and meet small challenges. A steep mountain road, Cherry Springs Hill, rose a few miles south of my cabin. The first time I attempted this long climb, I ground out 200 yards before dropping wobbly-kneed and gasping to the pavement. Every day I attacked it with new determination and got a little farther. Each time I perfected my experiments in breath control, muscle fatigue, and energy conservation to notch another hundred yards or so. Weeks went by. Maybe months. At long last I took the hill in a single pull. I never stopped short again.

Over the next few years I bicycled to all corners of Pennsylvania and beyond. One windy autumn I cut diagonally across the state, up and down the Blue Mountains, long hauls and steep, to spend a couple days at the Hawk Mountain Sanctuary, a nature preserve along the Kittitinney Ridge, where avian raptors of all varieties pass breathtakingly close to hawk watchers on craggy lookouts. There is nothing in my experience that rivals hawk-watching for the natural equivalent of buying a lottery ticket. It reads like this: " A boon is about to be granted to you from somewhere in the blue sky; it is winging quickly in your direction; it will bless you."

I biked to many places in the state of New York including New York City. But the longest trip was to Toledo, Ohio, my place of birth, then the home of my mother and of my earliest recollections, the latter always sacred, no matter what else you might think of the physical place. The trip was about 350 miles and took me three days. The first day I put in 150 miles and stopped, leg-weary and wound down, in the southern tier of New York State, near Lake Chautauqua.

Here I committed a crime which, I now confess, was a commonplace on my longer trips. I stole onto the screened-in front porch of an off-season lake cottage to spend a comfortable night on a porch sofa rather than on the damp, lumpy ground. Technically, this was 'breaking and entering' or some such trifle, and I imagined I would spend a night or two in jail if I were caught at it. But I took care not to damage anything and drifted off to sleep comfily imagining that if only I were born thirty years earlier, I would be riding the rails with all my fellow hoboes.

I mentioned the attach-a-pants invention above. This was only one feature of my minimalist approach to long distance biking. To watch me pedal by you might think I was dashing around the corner rather than on a two hundred mile trek. I had no packs or panniers or saddle bags. All the gear I took, apart from a tiny tool kit tucked under the seat, was slung on a rope strung between the handlebars. That gear consisted of: the pants bottoms, four safety pins, a sweater (which doubled as a washcloth/towel), a pocket knife and plastic fork, toothbrush, and a few dollars for food. All of this was folded into a cotton blanket and a sheet of clear plastic that served as a sheath tent on cool or rainy nights. The rope doubled as a belt if I ever found myself in a social situation that asked for a belt. Food I bought as near to my stop as possible and only as much as I ate there. I never carried water. In those days you could drink out of springs or even small streams without a second thought. At least I never thought twice. Nor did I ever get sick.

I digress to examine Theory #46: Optimum Mode-of-Travel. This theory postulates a balance between the two critical variables operant while traveling through a landscape: visual interest and opportunity of observation. An ideal pace changes the scene rapidly: I am not bored. But not too rapidly: I *see* what is passing by. Walking seems a trifle slow to me, the view doesn't change fast enough to keep the eye, the working mind fully engaged. Car travel is way too fast, you miss practically everything. Bicycling strikes a happy medium. Not only does the visual field change at a lively clip, but you have the leisure to take it all in, and, if need be, just stop and look.

One of my travel mode experiments involved roller skates. As a kid I was fond of roller skating around our neighborhood in Toledo, Ohio. I was never an elegant skater, but the hours spent on mastering the steep, tricky incline of our driveway gave me the confidence that I could tackle anything.

I bought a pair of clamp-on skates at the Galeton Hardware with visions of skating into town for a loaf of bread, a screwdriver, or just for fun. I fancied this new mode would give me a fresh perspective on the changing scene, moving a little slower and without the need for maneuvering the bike. But the first trial exposed my miscalculation. The macadam surface of a rural Pennsylvania road is far rougher than that of Toledo city sidewalks. The first one hundred yard dash down West Branch Road left my brain so jiggled I had no composure to take in the scene. Later I did find fifty-yard patches of smooth skating on the road where I could have a little fun, but the grand experiment, the relaxed skate into town, was never realized.

I came to love serious music in high school (Campion Jesuit High, in Prairie du Chien Wisconsin, long since buried in strangers' memories and now, prophetically, a state prison) when a dorm mate brought in a hi-fi record player and a few LPs of Beethoven and Tchaikovsky. But my feeling was nurtured at a remove. In the years following I never picked up a musical instrument, never learned to read a score. Then I bought a cello a few weeks before my final exams in Göttingen. I acquired the instrument from a classically trained musician retired from the local orchestra. I remember him inquiring with a note of despair whether I intended to play 'yazz' on the instrument. I assured him I had no such intention. The truth was I hadn't the faintest idea what I was doing.

I never took lessons for the cello. I read one book of instruction, a tedious German treatise belaboring the precise angle with which to hold the bow, etc. So I was left to my own devices, to practice. I practiced a little in Germany; a little in Paris, where I lived after my Grand Tour; in Barcelona and the Canary Islands, where I spent the following winter. At my cabin in the woods I fooled with folk ditties, pieced out some seasonal songs, and labored over a few of the simplest pieces from Bach's <u>Unaccompanied Cello Suites</u>. But mostly, I improvised. From the point of view of a professional musician, my playing was an abomination - I loved it.

À l'instument (sic) du Maître

À l'instument du Maître J.S.

    I little understood at the time that I was to be involved in music as much as writing for the rest of my life. Not only that I married a musician but I feel melodies as deeply as words. I keenly sense the life in both and the realm common to them. The difference is that I have a certain facility with words, none with tones or melodies. I write sentences without noticing, but struggle to notate the simplest melodies which course through me every day when hiking trails or waiting for sleep. I would make a great subject for a masters thesis: "Inspiration vs Craft in Artistic Production: A Case History."

At my Pennsylvania cabin music played as everyday a role as the written arts. The Heath Kit hi-fi system I had built on a high school summer vacation served me well for playing my modest LP record collection, mainly Beethoven and Bach, with a sprinkling of Romantics and moderns, some jazz, mostly bartered acquisitions from college roommates. And I had the radio. By some quirk of atmospherics I picked up no local stations (if there were any) and few regional clear channels, like New York or Philadelphia. But Canadian stations, from the Maritimes to the Prairies, came in clarion. So I heard a lot of Saturday night hockey games on the French network and a goodly share of Glenn Gould, including his later experiments in contrapuntal verbal music, the *Solitude Trilogy*. This profoundly influenced my sense of prose as melody, music as subtext of speech, though I could not have said very much about it at the time. In retrospect, every play I've written, all of my prose pieces, have an implicit musical score, sometimes known to me, more often not.

Sonata #1, the So-called Divine Sonata

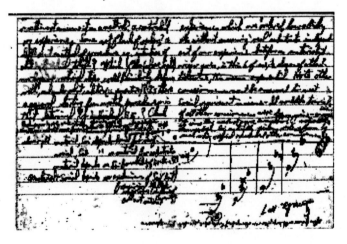

After I lost my Göttingen cello in the fire at my cabin, I acquired another a few months later, but the experience was never the same. I slacked off in my improvisatory exercises and stopped writing down my bicycle seat inspirations. Two decades later I had an automobile accident that among other things, crushed some of the joints in my left hand, and my cello playing days were over. According to me, but not according to cellist David Darling whom I met at a workshop at Bard College in the late '80's. He encouraged me to keep playing - bowing on open strings, pizzicato, anything - just keep playing. But I didn't.

In developing my own style of playing music I discovered it's not so important if confusion reigns between one's early explorations and their final expressions. In fact final expressions are rarely realized. It's the exploration that survives, if only in your treasured memory, the best place after all.

Here are some treasured memories:

My first winter I needed a ritual for the end of the year and hadn't yet created any of my own. So, I shoveled off a foot of snow outside my doorway to uncover a forest of seedlings of many species. I choose an eastern red cedar, a few inches high, and carefully dug it up, roots and all. I brought the fragile treelet into my cabin and arranged it somewhat ceremoniously in the middle of the floor of my tiny cabin. I wrapped the earth-clotted roots in an old tee-shirt and adorned the branches with tinsel of tree-moss and real icicles. Late in the evening I set my chair a foot away, picked out the melody of *Silent Night* on my cello, and played it again and again to the warming seedling. This was Christmas Eve. The next morning I replaced the tiny tree in its own cavity in mother earth and covered it with the same foot of snow, to wait until spring and its other life.

Or this: a scribbled note from a 'tween time asleep/ awake: "Before my mind becomes cluttered with the daylight rattle and flying confetti of waking up, I want to say - Perhaps I should not write any more poems, so artful in knowledge and practice. Ah, I will sing songs at which I am inept and beautiful yet. Before forever I may exhaust my ignorance, which physicians call death."

Or this: I play the prelude of Bach's D Minor Suite into the dead quiet February night and listen to the responding great horned owl.

Responding to my song? Probably not. Responding to the song of life? Could be.

And finally this: My real life as validated fantasy. I distinctly remember wanting to play my cello some humid midnight in a canoe on Sanctuary Pond where we lived in the eighties. Less distinctly do I remember if I ever did that. The image burns so vividly with yearning that I can easily believe I did, admit to it, constate it. So I DID do that. As much as I swam there, boated, skied and skated there. Never mind whether in a different experiential quadrant. Even less distinctly: Did I have a similar vision of playing my cello to the evening beavers? And then . . . did I? 'Yes' and 'No' fuse in this yearning dreamscape.

Listening, listening, listening at my post
For all the sounds I've always heard and never -
All the birds circling distant trees...
The farthest bird.. his song.. his wings...
The rack and moan of the highest trees,
The rushling wind through it, curling above...
Above that...
the loftiest air's whispering at space.
Then, strain, you, to catch
The whistling of stars in their speeding
And from infinitely beyond
Within the bounds of me
The hallooing of angels
Ineffably attenuate -
Souls of long silent songs are they, divined...
Were not the rasping of the grass growing round me
Deafening

Every day at my cabin was a fresh page. I explored realms I had no time for in my academic life, my life up to this point. I read writers no science curriculum would suffer: Joyce, Balzac, Kafka, Zola; and explored regions beyond my known world: Jung, Spencer, Santayana, Bergson. It was a time of revelation, of saying "Ah, a person can think *that*, too!" "Yes, *this* is another way to live life." I read

Thoreau's Walden for the first time and was impressed, not with his stay in the woods - I was doing a more thorough job of that than he - but with his breathtaking insights into the grand enterprise of life and his gift of saying so, one word after the other.

I expanded my thin familiarity with the European novels: Flaubert, Fielding, Diderot, Goethe, Sterne, Dostoevski but never quite got through Proust. The shorter works of Kleist, Rimbaud, and Nabokov filled the spaces in between.

My Allegheny Pierian Spring was the Galeton Lending Library which I visited every time I went to town. I don't remember taking down any books from the shelves of the one-room library except from the local history section. But I sucked dry its interlibrary loan service, which gave me access to every library book in Pennsylvania.

By day I biked the roads, by evening I hiked the forest trails, by night I invented melodies on my cello to capture the beauty of the day. But through all these times, I wrote. I wrote field notes that never got off the odd scraps they were scribbled on, pithy philosophic maxims on note cards piled under my desk, brief stories that filled yellow legal pads stacked in a corner, and grim allegories on the harried lives of wild animals. The animals might have been a school of nursery trout trapped in their synapses or a ruffed grouse agonizing over each moment's decision to freeze or flee. These creatures bore a more than fleeting resemblance to me.

Letters are warmer numbers, a little more red and blue,
Words too, orange and more violet than their sum of letters
Burgeon lusher, madder fleeter
Poem incarnadine, viridescent growth -
Inscrutable peer and seed of number.
Tranquil now in this declension, divining ecstasy close by,
I reach to savor
One . . . a poem moment number

63

Looking back I see the design of my being there evolved from initial self discovery to exploration of a dual world: the imaginative and the natural. My writing more and more took the form of expressing one in terms of the other, not always in the same direction. It seems now irrelevant whether my writings possessed literary merit or philosophical cogency. They were mine, they were me, I was happy scribbling them/me out. Writing, in those halcyon days, was a love labor. I labored upon myself, and loved peeling off layers, discovering what I believed. What I believed is what I wrote. Samples of what I wrote are scattered through this memoir and in the Appendix.

I had come to the woods to recover whatever of myself was buried under the expectations of others, some long since dead. Much of this work I carried out unconsciously - hiking, biking, making music - but also by writing. The longer I stayed at my hermitage the longer my stories grew and from my current perspective less interesting. They expanded from poems to snappy, one page Kafkaesque parables, to Kleistian short-shorts, to longish short stories in the manner of Nabokov, a play or two under the influence of Büchner, finally a picaresque novel, Jamie, the Neo-Manichean, an answer of sorts to Jacques, Le Fataliste, featuring a pair of improbable characters bicycling through Western Pennsylvania. Once again, each of the two heroes looked more like halves of me than any whole person. When I decided to offer the novel for publication, the idyll was over, the present subject was for the moment exhausted. If I were to write more, I needed to take in more of the world beyond myself.

My happy-go-lucky philosophizing about the nature of reality was moving on a parallel track. My interest in first questions began in college, where I gave a seminar on the deniability of the principle of contradiction, using as a counter-example a phenomenon from the physics of fluids. I smile now at my naiveté . . . but I still think I was right.

The concept 'Not' is a confused notion, relative mainly to sweaty seeking and sweatier desiring. For example; 'My socks are not here' expresses only a sordid frustration, nothing more. Your socks are somewhere, that is the positive reality. Dwell on it. If, indeed, your socks are not anywhere, you don't have any socks and the lament 'My socks are not here' is gibberish, not worth translating into dog-barks.

None the less, the statement 'My socks are not here' refers only to material socks, socks under the old dispensation. You certainly have possible socks and they are everywhere, they choke the universe. Muse over your possible socks, they are infinitely more interesting than your material socks, and you may even discover that you don't need your old-dispensation socks, you don't even want them.

I spent years in the exegesis of the cardinal insight of my last days in Göttingen: that science was not *the* answer to the human mind's root question, but one of many passable answers. I studied Aristotle's <u>Organon</u>, Roger Bacon's <u>Novum Organum</u>, making copious notes toward my own <u>Novissimum Organum</u>.

<u>Novissimum Organum</u>, according to my notes at the time, was conceived as something larger than a writing, more a Way Forward. 'I will raise a monument more lasting than bronze, called NO'. A mind shifting enterprise. just as Bacon with his <u>Novum Organum</u> laid the foundation for the scientific age. NO was to be the answer to the big question; What Is it All About Now?

Another of my hobby horses (rented from Bergson) at the time was an examination of the notions: discreta *vs* continua, *i.e.* separate vs inseparable entities. The wisdom of the past three thousand years was to look more closely at continua and discover the discreteness of them - time, space, matter, notions, souls. I prophesied the next three thousand years would look less closely at the piles of unrelated debris thus generated and recognize their smooth continuity. This movement had already begun. To sound the trumpet, I made a provisional list of entities that may prove to be one rather than many:

List of Continua (1965):

God - Man	*Me - Author - Hero -*	*Past - Present - Future*
New - Old	*Reader - You*	*Individual - Society*
Matter - Spirit	*Conscious - Unconscious*	*Particle - Wave*
Genes - Environment	*Reality - Fantasy*	*RNA - DNA*
Yes - No	*Received - Created*	*Personal-Racial Memory*
True - False	*Aristocracy -Bourgeoisie-*	*This - That*
Male - Female	*Proletariat*	*Continua - Discreta*

Where was I headed with my philosophizing? Was this the culmination of my thinking and feeling from that fateful October afternoon at Wilhelm Weber Strasse 10? How ironic that despite my surviving pile of scribbled notes about NO, I never actually wrote it, at least I don't remember doing it and haven't found the manuscript. Ramping up to write my Tome of Tomes was all I needed to complete the mission I was on, the nudge forward was the whole of it.

My life, my inner life at any rate, was mythic, mythopoetic. With that new sense of *myth* I discovered MYTH and greedily devoured Bullfinch, Eliade, and Campbell. I had something to say of myth, but I never said it to anyone but the chipmunks. This is another way to tell your story, but how much could the little rodents have cared, busy as they were with real acorns.

> *Life isn't about finding yourself.*
> *Life is about creating yourself.*
> *- George Bernard Shaw*

I pored over Locke, Berkeley, and Hume and their intellectual descendants, Santayana, Bergson and Quine. I was preparing another summation, an ethical upshot to NO: Make Your Own World, a manifesto in this case never even framed, and no surprise! In what ecosystem could such a revelation breathe? A testament to my doggedness, I still wrestle with these problems: a few years ago I wrote a play based on the book, The Philosophy of As If.

Digression #7f: In my woodsy retreat I never ran across the name Hans Vaihinger, the author of The Philosophy of As If. I had steeped myself in the British skeptical tradition of Locke-Berkeley-Hume. Their arguments that we "know" much less than we assume we know have never been refuted, despite heroic attempts to save philosophy for philosophers, *e.g.* Kant, the Christian apologist, successor to Aquinas. Vaihinger, whom I read a few years ago while researching Einstein's philosophical beliefs, answered the question that was left hanging at the end of the eighteenth century: What do I really know; what do I imagine I know? I am amazed that Vaihinger is not a household name, at least in philosophical households. Vaihinger formalized what to some people is intuitively obvious: we fabricate our own world from the spare colored patches and sound scraps that we really 'know', our immediate givens. All the rest is fiction in the etymological sense, fabricated, made up, invention. He called the products of this invention "useful fictions", and included herein the material world, other minds, science, religion, mathematics, you name it. 'Useful' is admittedly an understatement here, we would be utterly non-functional as human beings without a rock-solid, unexamined acceptance of these inventions. 'Unexamined', however, is the key word. Questioning this acceptance requires an intellectual headstand: How long can you hang there? Could there be, on the other hand, a more apt philosophy for a solipsistic hermit?

My first reaction to reading Vaihinger (in C. K. Ogden's translation - the original is unreadable, what people make fun of in Teutonic scholarship) was a fist-pumping: Yes!! This is what I intuited years ago: we live in a fog and call it sunshine. Later, I softened. How winning, we humans! Forget that we know nothing and pretend we know everything. Look at it from the other end: despite knowing nothing we have the temerity to believe we know everything. Through the most desolate state of crushing ignorance, we *will* to stand upright. The gesture is heroic! Celebrate, sing our song!!

Recalling my veneration of the Theory of Fictions puts me in mind of the following: I have a lively sense of myself as a dodger, and not even an artful one. Maybe everybody feels this at some level of consciousness and I shouldn't fret about it. Indeed I don't greatly, but whenever in idle moments I review certain passages of my life, the sense becomes acute. For instance my academic career at Göttingen, Germany was so filled with bilingual misunderstandings and left-handed dealings with the regulations, I wonder that I emerged with a degree at all. I entered graduate school in ecology at SUNY New Paltz without so much as a high school biology course in my background, again through a combination of fast talking and sloppy listening. Then I was admitted to the Doctoral Program for Public Policy at New York University with perhaps mechanical engineering as my closest legitimizing background to that nebulous field. Later I taught a graduate level course in economics at Bard College, never having sat through Econ 101 or anything before or after. I never lied about my record but they never asked. One reads periodically of the autodidact brain surgeon caught at it, to the acute embarrassment of the hospital. I feel a great kinship with the charlatan. But nobody ever hauled me before the ethics board and I wonder whether there are such things in the real world. Does everyone have as rich a shadow life as I do? I wisely don't ask.

As a feckless attempt to capture some flavor of my thinking in those days, I submit a collection of aphorisms culled from my yellowed index cards:

I am time, rather than space or matter - not hours and years but from now to now. Live this.

The social world is heavily involved with the received myth and must be temporarily abandoned for the sake of the air and light you need to regenerate your own world.

Fear of the unpredictable is the driving force of systems-making - from a baby first stretching out its finger to Einstein's general field equations.

A true religious sense is the uneasy feeling that some profoundly important reality is absent from the seeming of things, the current account given of the world.

There are some memories that bring tears to the eyes with laughing, others that are greeted by knee-slaps until it hurts, and then those, so unbearable, you have to escape them, somehow.

You are never totally free of the received, the goal is the striving.

And that's what I gained at Galeton: the assurance I was conscious and striving in a direction, my direction.

I have covered at length what I gained in my stay in the Allegheny Mountains. Time to mention what I lost . . . that is, what I know I lost. What I don't know I lost would fill another volume but would have to be written by someone else.

I do know that I lost social skills. When I reentered the everyday world, I must have come across like Kaspar Hauser, the 19th Century German wolf boy. A general bumbling befell me, especially with commonplaces whose context I had to relearn from scratch. Routine speech forms such as "How ya doin' today?" or "What's up?" tripped me up. If someone asked me this, I would laboriously work up an analysis of my existential situation - to their obvious consternation. This of course was how I answered the question to myself, my principal communicant for years.

The social niceties were a labyrinth to retrace. For instance at the apple farm, where I later worked, I found myself greeting co-workers with a bright "Good Morning!" or "Hello there!" repeatedly, several times before lunch. No one said anything about it; they didn't have to.

The picture of me as Kaspar strolling into Nuremberg is perhaps best painted with the following story. In the mid-sixties I received a notice from my Toledo draft board to report for a physical, prior to my induction in the U.S. Army. I am proud to be an American and willing to defend my rights when they are threatened. Viet Nam was no such case. Like everyone I knew at the time I did not want to go to Nam. In fact I had continued my post graduate education in part for the love of learning and in part to carry the treasured 2S Selective Service designation: "Still in school, too important for National Defense to get shot at." After Göttingen and no longer loving formal learning, I finagled a letter from the Admissions Department of the University of Barcelona that affirmed I was technically admissible, which I agreeably translated for the draft board: "Señor Stapleton is virtually a student and, by the way, essential to Spain's survival as a freedom-loving country." For some reason the draft board didn't believe it. They sent me the conscription letter shortly thereafter. What to do? My college friends accessed an arsenal of tactics for avoiding this sentence: trucking up to Canada, kissing the sergeant on duty, shlucking one or more easily obtainable pills. My best friend spent the better part of his physical exam shuddering helplessly.

I vowed I would carry out no such deception. Not that I am Honest Abe, incapable of deceit. I lie as readily as anyone, as cheaply. No, this was a question of Principle. I had every reason to believe that the U.S. Army would want nothing to do with the likes of me, once they heard my story. It remained to tell that story. I told it first to a Detroit psychiatrist, a friend of a friend. What happened at that session is the funny part. As for the rest: no, the army did not want me; I never went to Viet Nam.

In keeping with my vow to tell it straight to the psychiatrist and the army, I paid special attention to my physical presentation, the way I looked and acted. I could have shown up in the shabby rags I lived in, I had plenty of them. No, I wanted to look normal, like everybody else in mid-twentieth century middle America. My story alone would carry the day. So I carefully dressed with that in mind, a super normal American guy circa 1965.

The shrink ended up agreeing I was not military stuff (no sane person has ever thought otherwise), but it was his report to the United States Army that remains seared in my memory. The memo was sprinkled with damning phrases: "Subject has tendency to blather . .

." (see 'How ya doin'?' above), and " . . . entertains a bizarre phantasy world." (I outlined for him my philosophy of life), but the kicker for the army was no doubt "Subject suffers from an incipient schizophrenic diathesis". I looked it up, it means 'tendency'. Now here's the good part: as an afterthought, the psychiatrist tossed in the phrase: "He dresses very oddly". This stunned me! After my heroic effort to reclaim normalcy! It would have almost been worth going to Nam, to have my attempt to be a regular guy validated. Almost.

Everyone
in some small sacred sanctuary of the self
is nuts.
-Leo Rosten

There is another area of loss, one more ambiguous than bumbled social encounters. In walking into the woods I effectively gave up a professional life. I never had a sustained career. I didn't understand this at the time, not that it would have changed my course. My longest professional involvement was the eight years I did environmental research at Hudsonia. For the rest I muddled through, patching together short-term teaching jobs or writing myself into six-month grants, quitting anything as soon as I became slick at it.

Would I have wanted a career? I admit to an occasional wistful twinge, the same sweet-sad 'It might have been . .', prefixed to 'children', 'fast cars', or 'a Nobel science prize', foregone possibilities that would have brought certain kinds of life satisfactions. I earned a Ph.D. in my fifties to satisfy one such lingering itch left over from my Göttingen days, when such an achievement seemed the best thing possible. I had no intention of using the degree for any career advancing purpose, I simply felt it belonged to me.

So the question remains: knowing what I know now, would I have . . ? And the answer is clear: no. For one, I refuse to regret any well considered decision of the past, no matter how badly it turned out. For the rest I ask myself: would that steady, settled life have lifted me, my soul, above the everyday? I think not. And that's my measure of a well lived life.

Here's something else that occurs to me. Yes I lost a professional life and I lost a social life in some usual sense, but I also lost a conventional life. Again it comes down to trade-offs: What's the cost-benefit ratio of living a conventional life? It's not easy to calculate on paper, black-on-white, but everybody has their own interior number. Mine is very high. A conventional life isn't worth a damn.

Last and least in my reckoning of losses during my long stay in the woods was my ignorance of pop culture, Americana. I read no newspapers in my time there, saw no television, listened to the radio very selectively and never to anything like a news broadcast. I literally did not know what was going on in the world while I was living in the Alleghenies, the mid-sixties to early seventies. I learned in the eighties about the great cultural upheaval of "The Sixties". Young people, it was said, were 'tuning in and dropping out'. Oh.

At the time I felt it was a good thing to be blissfully out-of-touch with American culture, which I conflated with television. I remain to this day blissfully out-of-touch with television. We don't have one and won't. In our household, 'TV' stands for 'Turkey Vulture'. But I wonder now about the loss of communion with my own kind, the field of shared knowledge with compatriots, which for me has mile-deep holes. Friends start talking about rolling stones or this-or-that episode on "The Boat of Love" and I smile wanly and, I hope, knowingly. I have no idea what they're talking about. Here is a region of discourse where I might as well be Armenian or Martian. And that's the rub: I've become less sanguine in my Armenian role, to say nothing of the Martian.

Before my serial epiphany I suffered through a number of bad choices, mostly others' choices. Learning to follow my own nose did not exempt me from more bad choices, but I've had the sense they were *my* choices, I can live with them. Now and then I envision my deathbed review and will be able to say: I did what I wanted to do; I didn't hurt anybody, at least willfully; I regret only this and a bit of that; I lived fulfilled.

By the end of eight years I had done what I had come to do. I left my idyll not in the hot rush that I came to it, but in halting stages, taking off for weeks to New York with friends or to Colorado with my sister Mary and her robust family. Then months to test which kind of farm work I was best suited for - haying for a Galeton neighbor, dairying for a New York family, or apple farming in a Hudson Valley orchard - before discovering I was suited for none of the above. I don't have the competence to run a farm. I ended this interlude at The Mohonk Preserve near New Paltz, NY, where I agreeably helped Dan Smiley band birds, press flowers, and make sense of his sixty years of natural history records.

At Mohonk I learned that the West Virginia Pulp and Paper Company intended to sell the land my cabin was sitting on and asked me to remove the building. I returned with two friends to the Allegheny woods, dismantled the cabin, and reconstructed it at Mohonk's Duck Pond where I had been living in a tent. When I left Duck Pond a few years later, the cabin was again dismantled and moved. God knows where it is now, long since recycled or returned to earth.

I do not miss the dwelling of my high days, I rarely wonder how it fared. My material environment never did impinge much on my inner life. I have never named a car or axe that I owned, my life moves from insight to insight, rather than from house to house. Still, pieces of my Galeton *ménage à un* stayed with me for the next few years: the stove served as the only, but inadequate heat source for the much larger house at the Burroughs Sanctuary. The new cello followed the stove and played duets with a violin, wielded by a friend in the Hudson Valley, until the latter, a luthier by trade, helped me sell the cello to a promising student in Kingston, NY; the chair-bed was donated to the Salvation Army when we relocated to the Pacific Northwest years later; the harpsichord, half devoured by mice during my multi-year absence, ended in a friend's firewood stack. And the kitchen table? I can only imagine that it was bolted by bacteria one humid summer evening when I wasn't looking.

Has anything survived from those times? A Solingen kitchen knife I bought upon my arrival in Göttingen, 1959; a few half burned books; boxes of writings and a handful of photos to sift out of attic boxes when I publish these memories. What else? Looking back, I see my time at the cabin as a gift, a lifelong permission to stop at any point and ask myself "Who are you now? What are you doing? Is that worth doing?"

That gift has served me well . . . and it has disrupted my life in many ways. But the time at my Pennsylvania hermitage remains a lodestar for the rest of my life.

Bloodroot

Not often a soft evening
Moment empetals my stamen soul
From the noise of expecting
Remembering and the cold of stars,
Dreaming in its dark
Perfume and aware as a flower
Of life.
Not often
But now

APPENDIX OF STORIES

SILVERSTEIN OR UNFROZEN POETRY

Out here I hear about things late, or more usually, not at all. This news clipping I'm holding now - the dateline is two weeks ago. The news bodies are certainly long since done with the item, except perhaps in some jungle compounds and even the commentators and analysts have finished kneading from it the juices they pretend are there. All that over, I feel I can now savor it without constraint - in my own space as it were and smile at it absently on trade-wind summer evenings. I particularly like this item because it expresses in its way something I have mused about off and on for many years, though I could never dream of saying it in words or telling it with a gesture, even by a look in my eyes at an unconscious moment. This is its richness to me, a secret content the pundits would not have known to tap.

"In the Capitol City of X, the famed architect, Silverstein, gave testimony at a hearing attempting to uncover evidence concerning the huge bomb placed by persons unknown in the sub-basement of the Department of the Exterior, the latest and last of Silverstein's commissioned series of public works for the Capitol City. His testimony, as follows, was confused and wholly irrelevant to the question at hand:

'There are words to talk about public buildings,' he began, 'to exhaust them completely, especially at the official opening, because everything in them and about them was on a blueprint, well-labeled and with accompanying descriptions in formally correct English. All this goes to the contractor, to the foreman, to the workers. They use every word and nothing is left unsaid, so that at the opening, no piece of furniture is out of place, no paper folded or pencil tipped in a way not fully described. Then all the many visitors see precisely the same things, the things that are everybody's to see with their same eyes, are constrained to say the same things, use those very words, blueprint words, the words fixed to a public building.

'How different it is in the shambling hovel on a recluse island, where there are no words, were no words when it was thrown together from logs, stones, and palms in a mindlessly felt need for shelter. All the more so now that each corner has its own soul of a flower growing there among its six unnamed things in the darkness of years, the table shifted unconsciously more this way for comfort and that

dirty rag stuck into the hole in the floor. There are no words for the places or things in my home. 'Wretched' or 'quaint' or 'homey' or something in the focusing eyes of the rest. To my inner eye, unplumbably meaningful, wholly ineffable. Finding no word to say, that's what's growing in my corners, there . . . . For my part I would rather see my wordable, little-significant arrangements of public buildings rise in an insensible dust and spread over the city that each may see them with his inner eye and mould it to the shape of his own soul, sensing in it the things that are solely his.'

"The investigating committee did not press Silverstein on specific points. They seemed frankly relieved to see him leave the stand, all the more so in light of his announced intention to resign the post of Chief Architect and return to his island retreat in the South Atlantic.

"The bomb was discovered in time and defused though it was impossible to remove it, even in the near future. It was set to explode when the building would be empty and not yet housing any Department files. A grand international scheme of sabotage seemed out of the question.

"The contractor's evidence was more coherent but no more enlightening. It was beyond his comprehension how such a monstrous device could be smuggled into the building during any phase of the construction without his knowledge, and certainly not without highly sophisticated machinery. He calculated the integrally situated bomb would have pulverized this building of novel design without seriously damaging any of the surrounding structures. The investigation was closed and the matter dropped."

Thus far the news story. The commentaries probed deeper, of course. They lauded Silverstein's many years of dedication to the expression of the nation in the beauty of its architecture, played upon the earned right of repose and retreat for the twilight years of an artist of such national prominence, earned through years, possibly overworked years in the service of his country. All enthusiastically greeted the summary closure of the investigation into the regrettable matter. Each too had some individual observations to make, many words of them in fact, which served mainly to set off the advertising in the newspapers. None mentioned, which they all evidently believed, that Silverstein - senile, over-wrought, half-crazed or what - had placed the bomb himself in some ecstasy of diverted genius. Designed it in fact so

76

subtly into the sub-structure that the contractor, a literal-minded, self-assured fool, could not have imagined he was installing it with his own machinery.

Must I say it? I am moved by this account because it helps me sense something suddenly that I could not tell in a thousand years, and then again because I am Silverstein. Bang!

BIRDS . . . PEOPLE

Once upon a distant dawn, when forests were virginal, all the birds met in the fine new growth of a tall pine. At the same time the people held a conference upon the massy roots of a broad oak. The birds had come to decide whether words or music were better for them as had the people.

There was not much agreement: the parrots and mynahs articulated their grand notion of the nobility, distinction, and utility of speech and at some length; the nightingale sang her song. The crows tended to agree with the parrots, but kept a wary eye cocked for any advantage to come their way. The goshawks looked at the chickadees so attentively, some thought it violated the truce. The eagles looked majestic but at no one in particular. Soon it became apparent that no agreement was in sight and the night-birds were becoming sleepy. The night-birds were much admired for all their qualities and the meeting was postponed to dusk.

Meanwhile, below, the people had decided that words were better for them. The night-people may have felt differently, but they lay curled asleep among the scented roots. And they were not much admired.

At dusk the birds returned to alight around the lofty top. The warblers sang well in the gloaming as they do; the parrots blinked. Not much was said. After a while the birds flew off singly - some to sleep, some to sing of the wonder of nights, many silently happy for the serenity of it.

MY SALAMANDERS

On the unused railroad grade that runs behind my cabin the salamanders creep around on cooling summer evenings. They're two to three inches long and range from bright orange after a heavy rain to dark brown in the dry season. I'm worried sick about them. I like to take short walks there in the quiet evenings or even after dark to ease the tensions of a hectic day, but I usually come back more jittery than before, wondering how many of the little fellows I've stepped on. I couldn't be more careful, checking every foot placement, not stopping to rest for fear one of them might crawl through the loose gravel under my foot, maybe from behind, and the slightest shift of my weight would send his entrails squirting onto my other boot. I guess a lot of people would laugh at my worrying over such an insignificant animal . . . no, there is an answer and I think I know what it is: retrain the salamanders, simply re-educate them . . . my nightmares about running along a road made out of salamanders . . . maybe being squashed underfoot, quickly and forever, would be a salvation for them . . . so the plan I've worked out, a little schedule of lessons . . . probably won't do him any real harm and it could be fairly painful . . . he'll come to understand what I'm trying to teach him . . . and so on down the line . . . maybe starting to get a little stern wouldn't be the worse thing . . . going 'rrraaaggh', 'rrraaaggh, ragh', shoving that bullfrog right up to him . . . and I see already I'm not going to get away with being so humane . . . a few yards maybe, to make him understand at all costs and if he hits a tree halfway, well, he'll be spared whatever I think up for the next lesson . . . what makes me sleepless . . . and all the people after me who won't be able to walk there, relaxing . . . just better all the way around.

WHEN?

Dear human friends, wherever you may be, please hear us, take pity on our lot and help us. A grouse's life is a difficult one, wholly circumscribed by terrors, some real but most imaginary.

We grouse have a problem, an old problem stretching back to the time when grouse first became distinguishable from other forms of life, well before the arrival of men. Are you surprised? Grouse History is learned by every grouse, beginning almost before she pecks out of her shell, and is not laid aside until her dying day, yet so vast is the subject that were she to listen attentively to the gobbles and coos of the History her every free second - as indeed all grouse do - her highest hope at the end would be to understand she knew in essence nothing. Grouse History is the only what-you-might-call intellectual discipline that we grouse have developed, but it is not a theoretical study. It has only practical value. We live by the precepts established by our forefathers, the most ancient ones. It is just this tendency, or rather need, that has frozen us as we are through the ages. Still it has kept us alive, as many of us as there are.

Grouse are surely one of the most harried species on earth. Our predators and persecutors include, it seems to me sometimes, practically every species aware enough to notice us. Against these Nature has provided us with only two defenses: camouflage and flight. Actually not real defenses, no more so than our tendency to wish for the best while knowing the worst. We use our coloration by carefully choosing our feeding and roosting habitats, usually marshes or underbrush, always where the possibility of sudden flight is given in all directions. Now the crux of the problem: when the signal of danger is given or when there is some suspicion of danger or even and especially when there is not the slightest indication of it, it is our ancient custom to stand deathly still, trusting to concealment to save our lives. It must be frighteningly clear that at some point in the fatal approach, we must decide to let go our one claw-hold on a willowy safety and snatch at the other - lurch up, a terrified whistling of wings, crashing bramble - and fly away. Here the agonizing question, the central problem of our existence - When? When to start from concealment to flight? There's no third possibility, the only question is: When?

You are asking yourselves - 'Why us? Why humans?' Rather than one of the many other species who are closer to grouse in sensibility. Yes, it is surprising especially when there is a certain number among you - I believe you call them 'hunters' - who have made systematic ravages on us. Far from bearing grudges, however, we see the fruitlessness of picking at open, unhearable wounds. However much we long for peace in the animal kingdom and a reasonable security for all, we recognize this is an absurd wish, it will never come.

We chose humankind for several reasons: first we have noted that you are intelligent in your own peculiar way and that way includes making minute, exhaustive, written accounts of seeming trivia. Furthermore, from our own experience, this kind of work requires a breast reasonably free of panic and humans have always seemed to us to be - phlegmatic would be too hastily chosen a word here - rather even-tempered in their well-ordered workaday lives. But especially because we hope some few of you, concerned about the plight of other animals, would willingly help if only you saw a concrete way of doing so.

Why don't we grouse - who best understand our own problems, their complexity - undertake our own researches? Perhaps a few of my remarks have given you an inkling of the answer. The simple matter of fact is: we haven't the time. Does this strike you as strange, since in your terms we seem to accomplish nothing day and night? But that's only the way it seems, the opposite of the inner reality. Put yourselves for a moment in our place, crouched low among the reeds, watching and listening, mostly listening. Every breeze that sways the stalks means danger, every flick, dart, and shadow is imminent death, each crackle, sigh, and squeak is the first second of eternity in our wild beating hearts. 'Safety' is a word, like 'nothing', danger, death is what is. How many times has the realization frozen me in my tracks that there was absolutely no cause for alarm. We sleep so little. A welcome respite? If you had my dreams you wouldn't sleep at all. We have no time! It would be fatal to divert our attention for a second to analyze our situation.

Before you say you will help us let me give you some idea of the complexity of our situation. Try to put yourself in our place. At every sign of danger we are ready to fly off. Indeed our normal nervous state of expectant tension holds us at the very edge of flying every minute of the day and night. But to do so would be foolish, since flight is often more dangerous than concealment.

Suppose a twig snaps - Freeze! What was it, a cat behind me? A hunter with gun ready? Is it getting closer, quieter, circling, sneaking, waiting, breathing

81

hard, ready to jump, swoop, shoot, should I fly or freeze? Is the sky full of hawks, arrows, nets, buckshot? Will it pounce on me if I wait another second, will I be cut in two if I fly up now? Am I dead whatever I do? What is it thinking, does it even know I'm here, stalking, then waiting, grinning, tasting me already?

We don't hope for a solution, a real solution, nothing with the faintest flavor of finality. Should we breathe our thanks the problem is not getting worse, more complicated, more frightening? Despite our rank imagination, we can form no image how this might be the case. No, we must hope for something, anything. With your help some movement along the way, even a signpost pointing - pointing perhaps in several directions at once, even revolving - it would be a hope.

We realize the fruits of your researches will not be highly significant, actually not significant at all. Nevertheless, the word you will have for us after your study will come as a word of salvation, we will live by it. It won't be the 'final answer', we don't even have a word in our language for 'final answer'. But it will be our answer, whether ambiguous, impenetrable, or even irrelevant to the problem itself. We - half our lives are spent in the wilderness of the invented - have a place for such an answer.

But to our problem - When? Let me assure you the problem is only half what you are now thinking. When to forsake cover and take to flight. There is no inverse to this problem: when to leave off flying and seek cover. That is solved for us. Once we are frightened into flight - the whistling wings, the crazy lurch - we fly to exhaustion.

Oh can't you see our plight, feel it? If you could only tell us what instant, forget the whole problem of When? Just give us an instant. Never mind the researches, they would be meaningless anyway. Just an instant. What instant? Any instant! It doesn't matter anymore! The next instant that comes to your mind. Just say it and we'll do it, we'll do it forever, we'll do it for the sake of peace!

Not peace from others, they'll kill us anyway. Peace from ourselves!

MORE ABOUT THE AUTHOR

Jim Stapleton had a fairly conventional childhood in the 1940s and '50s in Toledo, Ohio. From there things went a little sideways: he left home for high school in Wisconsin, college in Michigan, and for his post-graduate work studied theoretical physics in Göttingen, West Germany. Returning to the U.S. in 1963 he spent the next eight years as a hermit, the subject of this book. Moving on, he worked on a series of farms, settled in the Mid-Hudson Valley, conducted ecological research at the Mohonk Trust, and pursued advanced degrees in biology and environmental science. In the 1970s and '80s he taught at various colleges (Bard, Vassar, and the New School for Social Research); and helped found Hudsonia, a not-for-profit environmental research institute. Stapleton has written plays: "Henry & Emily", an imagined encounter between Thoreau and Dickinson, "Playing for Keeps", a love story, and "Tango As-If", a smash-up of an Argentinian dance style and German idealist philosophy. Recently, he published Sanctuary Almanac (available through Amazon.com), an account of his life as resident naturalist at the Burroughs Sanctuary in upstate New York. He lives now in the winsome Green Mountain village of Bristol, Vermont with his wife, Diana Bigelow, with whom he enjoys an engaging avocation in the theater.

www.jimstapleton.com